>>>> / **VIRTUAL MUSE** /

VIRTUAL MUSE

Experiments in Computer Poetry

Charles O. Hartman

WESLEYAN

UNIVERSITY

PRESS

Published by
University Press of
New England
Hanover and London

WESLEYAN UNIVERSITY PRESS

Published by University Press of New England, Hanover, NH 03755

Printed in the United States of America   5   4   3   2   1

CIP data appear at the end of the book

ACKNOWLEDGMENTS

"Monologues of Soul & Body" was first published in Tyuonyi, and later appeared in *Glass Enclosure* (Wesleyan University Press, 1995).

"Seventy-Six Assertions and Sixty-Three Questions" was published in Grist On-Line.

Sentences was published by Sun & Moon Press in 1995.

"Extraordinary Instruments" was published in TriQuarterly.

Also it must be carefully remember'd that first-class literature does not shine by any luminosity of its own; nor do its poems. They grow of circumstances, and are evolutionary.
Walt Whitman, "A Backward Glance o'er Travel'd Roads"

A poem is a small (or large) machine made of words.
William Carlos Williams

Poeta nascitur, non fit.

> > > > / **CONTENTS** /

Alice sets a stringent standard for authors when she pointedly inquires: What is the use of a book without pictures or conversations?

This book has no compelling pictures and only indirect descriptions of highly abstruse conversations. What *Virtual Muse* does have is this address on the World Wide Web:

http://www.conncoll.edu/ccother/cohar/programs/

Here you will find MacProse, a Macintosh version of the PROSE program described in chapter 7, ready to be downloaded and run. Key parts of the source code are also available, for those who'd like to tinker.

In the future, I hope to add other programs to this site once I have wrestled them into a usable state. (Programs written for research and experimentation tend to crash in annoying ways when used by anybody but their author.) These probably will include the DOS version of PROSE.

I hope the book makes it clear that—for me and I hope for interested readers—the point isn't the programs themselves (which are fairly simple and not particularly original) but the uses that can be made of them. For this reason, I will always include source-code files with comments on program structure so that more sophisticated programmers can easily alter them.*

---

*Readers may also want to visit the WebSite for the University Press of New England for information about its publications. http://www.dartmouth.edu/acad-inst/upne/

>>>> / **VIRTUAL MUSE** /

Talking about computer poetry is almost like talking about extraterrestrial intelligence: great speculation, no examples.

In the hundred-year history of computers, the most wild-eyed prophets have sometimes dreamed of a utopia in which man and machine (sexism reinforced by alliteration) debate on equal terms about the meaning of life and the relative merits of cells and circuits. Perchance they take the occasion to compose and exchange a few sonnets or maybe odes. Poetry in this distant dream serves as a kind of ultimate touchstone of intelligence. The ability to write poems is the talisman by which we'll know that computers have really *arrived*.

This use of poetry isn't surprising. Poetry has great prestige as the sign of Culture—which doesn't make everybody want to read it. When people are looking around for profound examples of what it is they, uniquely, as people, do, poetry gets conscripted as a time-honored and somewhat weary example. It doesn't usually suit people's purposes to define human uniqueness in terms of economics, prayer, torture, or the invention of the weekend.

Yet when poetry is treated as the hallowed repository of sacred Culture, it's dead. No poet worth reading really thinks of poetry as that. A culture worth belonging to has a present and a future, as well as a past. Poetry is something we *do* with language. Or rather, it's a lot of different kinds of things we do with language. It's a place where we can attend to language, as a stadium is a place to attend to the body. And language *is* something that defines people.

Throughout this book I'll be interested in the complicated boundary between what computers can do with language and what they can't. Obviously (since the book exists), I believe computers can do something worthwhile in the way of poetry. Which brings me back to the first question: Why hasn't there been any computer poetry?

Well, there has—but not much. There was a computer program in California in 1962 that turned out poems. Its caretaker submitted some short verses to *Horizon* (a big glossy magazine mostly devoted to Culture) under the pen name "Auto-Beatnik." I haven't been able to find any later trace of the program or its author, one R. M. Worthy of General Precision, Inc. A couple of other quite similar experiments surfaced in the following ten or twenty years.

Two decades after Auto-Beatnik came *The Policeman's Beard is Half-Constructed* (1984), a book written by a program called Racter. Racter is short for "raconteur." The program's designers, William Chamberlain and Thomas Etter, were especially interested in getting the machine to tell stories and have conversations. At these terribly difficult tasks, Racter turns out tour de force performances—very impressive, very uneven:

> Bill sings to Sarah. Sarah sings to Bill. Perhaps they will do other dangerous things together. They may eat lamb or stroke each other. They may chant of their difficulties and their happiness. They have love but they also have typewriters. That is interesting.

A. K. Dewdney, the human reviewer of Racter's book for *Scientific American*, quoted this example to show, first, how "marvelously funny and even thought-provoking" Racter's productions could be, and then how nonsensical: "The allowances I have been making for Racter all along are stretched to the breaking point when Racter mentions that besides their love they also have typewriters. Invited to share in this extraordinary insight, I tremble on the brink of a completely unknown mental world, one that I would prefer not to enter." As it happened, when I read Dewdney's review, I had already picked this same passage as my favorite example of Racter's potential for profound serendipity. What was going on here?

Well, think about a writer married to another writer. Typewriters, until computers replaced them not so long ago, were to writers what scalpels are to surgeons. Writers are often cranky people, preoccupied, out of step with everything outside and around them. This makes them difficult to live with—which doesn't make them any better at living with each other. Successful marriages between writers are fairly rare. In the context of such a marriage, Racter's little story would ring loud and true; Bill and Sarah have love, but they also have typewriters.

For one reason or another (human beings lead rather inscrutable lives), Dewdney didn't feel the same resonance that I did. The "completely unknown mental world" that he "would prefer not to enter" wasn't just Racter's, it turns out, but mine as well. In this instance, the computer and I—and not Dewdney—had a meeting of minds.

Or to be more precise, I had the experience of a "meeting of minds," which Dewdney didn't have. There wasn't really a "mind" there for mine to meet. Yet if I were judging a poetry contest and came across Racter's piece, I wouldn't immediately toss it into the Reject pile, and I wouldn't immediately suspect it was a *merely mechanical production*. I might use that phrase to dismiss many other pieces from the book; but for that matter I might reject many of the human-authored contest poems in just the same terms (as Cowper did Alexander Pope's). It's important to distinguish "intelligence" like Racter's from real human intelligence, but it's not always easy, not if we go purely on products. If we peek inside the box—look at the program's source code, for example—we may dismiss the whole thing as a contraption. But if we could peek inside the human brain box (which brain science is beginning to do), we might have the same reaction. A neuron has no mind.

The search for understanding between computers and people leads through a denser forest than is usually suggested by the popular literature on "artificial intelligence." People discussing computer intelligence and language and communication have often assumed that we understand human intelligence, language, and communication a lot more straightforwardly than we do.

From one perspective, poetry is a subtle interactive business carried out between a poet and a reader. There are other perspectives, other definitions of poetry, but any theory that leaves out the reader's necessary interpretive genius (though it's often *unconscious* genius) fails to explain much. This means that the question "Is this poetry?" is often very interestingly difficult to answer. If Racter's story isn't poetry, why not? Because it's in prose? (Do we have any trouble agreeing that it's a story?) Because of its unexpected leaps of thought? Because it doesn't make *enough* leaps of thought? Because it isn't really thought at all, having been produced by a machine, unless William Chamberlain is pulling our leg, in which case, would it be satiric poetry? If it isn't poetry, where does it stop being poetry—somewhere in the middle, or at the end, or before we even read it?

The complexity of poetic interaction, the tricky dance among poet and text and reader, creates a game of hesitation. In this game a properly programmed computer has a chance to slip in some interesting moves. The brute-force effort to make a machine into a human poet seems doomed to death by boredom. A more promising attack concentrates on the open field where poems and readers meet. Readers intuitively deduce the existence (and the situation and feelings) of a poet. They do this through what is often the only evidence before them, the poem. This struggle to deduce, to interpret, leaves readers open, exposed, their lines extended, their own momentum propelling them headlong toward meaning.

Only poets, though, are likely to spot this opening. And only somebody with a modicum of programming experience (or with access to somebody who programs) is likely to find a way of exploiting it. The combination is unusual, which is why there has been so little computer poetry. As computers multiply explosively, the conjunctions are beginning to happen. Jackson Mac Low has been using a computer to automate poetic procedures for several years; Paul Hoover and others are exploring related topics. And the Internet sprouts ever more vigorous discussions of "hypertext," multiply linked on-line text.

Hypertext offers exciting possibilities as a way to present poetry, and more than that. Like any new medium, it will change the way poets write poems and readers read them. The typewriter gave poets more precise control over spacing on the page, which they learned to use to control the meanings of words. The printing press changed poetry's audience, which changed poetry. Writing itself had complicated effects on both the nature of poetry and its place among other kinds of verbal art.

(Robert Pinsky, one of the earliest literary hypertext authors, surveyed the state of affairs as of March 19, 1995, in "The Muse in the Machine: Or, The Poetics of Zork," in the *New York Times Book Review*. Later the same year, the University of Michigan Press published Michael Joyce's *Of Two Minds: Hypertext Pedagogy and Poetics*.)

Hypertext and its cousins represent "computer poetry" in one sense of the phrase. Yet these debates about a new medium for poetry's *presentation* haven't dealt much with the use of computers in the *composition* of poems. The work of Racter and Auto-Beatnik appeared on the old-fashioned page. This is "computer poetry" in a much different sense. By actually programming the computer to help to select and manipulate words, we can probe, even more intimately than with hypertext, into the poet's and reader's relation to language. This is the kind of project that I'll be exploring here. As we'll see, the question isn't exactly whether a poet or a computer writes the poem but what kinds of collaboration might be interesting.

So this book gives a report from the front: a firsthand account of some experiments in using computers to help write poems. It's a fragment of autobiography. This can be taken partly as a disclaimer. I won't be reviewing the latest developments in artificial intelligence or current research in generative linguistics. I'm not a professional programmer. I'm a poet, which is to say a "professional" in a field where "amateur" would be a fair synonym. Above all, I'm a person who likes to work in more than one area of thought at once. (These "areas" have been defined by convention. Crossing their borders isn't a crime against nature.) I've followed some lines of research in this double area—computers and poetry—a little farther than anyone else I know of. In the course of this work I've written several poems that I and other people have found valuable. Some poems are included in the Appendix.

Since this is autobiography, the rule is, *don't wait for final results*. In the future I may go beyond what I describe in these chapters, or my work may lead me off in new directions that have nothing to do with computers. What I offer here is a momentary cross-section: one poet's thought, at one point in history, about one corner of the art.

I'd like to thank the Ingram Merrill Foundation for a fellowship that allowed me to write the first draft of this book. Actually, the Foundation's intention was to support me while I wrote poems, and I hasten to add that I've *been* writing poems, very diligently and happily. I hope they won't mind that this book happened to come out too.

START WITH COMPUTERS

When my son can be trusted not to put jelly in the keyboard, and when he can tell an O from a o, I'll give him a computer. I'll probably need to, just to keep his hands off mine. He can use it to play games; it may help him learn to read; and soon he'll be writing programs that draw shapes, calculate primes, graph complex functions, and perhaps compose fugues. None of this, by itself, will make him a really unusual person. It may cost me less than I hear some toys do—something between a car payment and a month's mortgage.

I'm hardly the first person to notice that this represents a striking change from the world that produced his father just a few decades back. Computers are in and of our lives in ways that thirty years ago weren't even envisioned by science fiction writers. The reality of computers then, despite their fascinating history of conceptual victories, was too depressing to inspire the leap of fantasy it would have taken to imagine where we are now.

As a high school student in a college town, I heard about an evening class in computer programming that I could attend. I was moderately happy with mathematics and decided to try it. (We used to think programming was a kind of mathematics, rather than just a product of mathematics.) This would have been about 1963. The computer language was FORTRAN IV. I have no idea what kind of computer ran our class exercise programs because I never saw it. To some juvenile computer jockeys today, this may sound like a paradox; let me explain.

These were the bad old days of "batch processing." You wrote your little program to print all the prime numbers between 1 and

100— I mean you *wrote* it out on a piece of paper. Then you went in search of a free and functioning keypunch machine. This was a gray object the size of a pygmy hippopotamus, solidly packed with gears and motors and sounding like a broken beehive or one of those automated looms that were its collateral ancestors. (The Jacquard loom, developed between 1725 and 1745, was the first machine controlled by punch cards.) There you typed your program onto "IBM cards," one line per card. Then, after doing your best to weed out all the erroneous cards, you carried your "deck" to a plexiglass window, where the clerk, a grad student training as a computer acolyte, took charge of it. He (women were very scarce around computers) noted your job account number and entered your program into an interminable queue. The next day—or the next—assuming that the computer was "up" and not, as so often, "down" (it lived in some bombproof basement in a mythified cool glass chamber where all its attendants wore white, and its health was the subject of widespread anxiety and considerable superstition), you picked up your deck of cards wrapped in a thin bundle of wide green-striped printout paper that listed in several columns of incomprehensible code all the errors the computer thought you had made in your pursuit of a project whose intention it had clearly not understood in the first place. Like Sisyphus, the fellow rolling a rock uphill in Hell, you were free to reiterate this process as many times as it took.

Oddly enough, I found the experience of computer programming attractive in many ways, though certainly not enough to pursue it as a career.

In college, at the end of the same decade, I took a distribution-requirement course about computers. The language was still FORTRAN, programs were still processed in batches, and I still didn't know much about the machine itself or how it arrived at my little printout of error messages. Batch processing continued to enforce that aweful religious separation between the computer and the profane programmer. While the attraction was still there, the frustration held steady too.

In this course we were encouraged to choose our own final

projects. I was divided in soul and academic major between English and music, and I suppose I might have dithered between schemes for programs in those two areas. But in fact I don't remember contemplating even for a moment trying to deal with words. Computers didn't cope well with words at the time. The best programming language for the purpose, charmingly called SNOBOL, was a freak among its serious number-crunching relatives.

Instead, I wrote a program to harmonize chorales. My program would let me feed the computer the soprano melody of a Bach chorale, and the computer would write the alto, tenor, and bass voices to go with it. I worked out ways to encode all the rules for ensuring proper voice-leading, avoiding parallel fifths and octaves, encouraging contrary motion in the outer voices, and so on. There was even a random element, to introduce a bit of surprise into the harmonic progression. The input and output—the melody and the four-part harmonized chorale—took the form of lists of numbers that had to be translated back into notes by hand. Computers that could write (let alone read) musical notation were years and years away, even in advanced computer science labs.

I got a C+ on that project, which taught me, or should have taught me, a complex lesson. Though my program was correctly written, it wouldn't run within the tiny area of computer memory that the college had allotted for class projects. (I never knew the details of the inadequacy. Understanding them might have been beyond me anyway. Intimate knowledge of an operating system was very advanced stuff at the time.) My section teacher's evaluation, which I preserved in the file with my class notes in the vague hope of going back to the project someday, has enough exemplary historical interest to be quoted in full:

> While not being able to judge the musical quality or insight which you have demonstrated, I would say that as a computer project you have made a strategic error:
> Rather than aim for something which is realizeable, you have written a very complex and lengthy program, and as a result have not been able to run it and show that any of it works.

It would have been better to start with a small, working program and build on that.

Evidently you have mastered FORTRAN and I have no quarrel with your program as written.

In short, to borrow Howard Nemerov's line about some poets, I was a fine programmer—on paper.

One version of the lesson might have been that what counted in computer science was results, not beautiful fancies. Another version was that I was temperamentally unsuited to computer science. The idea of ironing out logistical details (especially in the nightmare hurry-and-wait world of batch processing) was not what attracted me to computers. The task of most computer professionals was, and still is, a management task; the talent of the best is a talent for getting things done. Design and innovation occupy a tiny percentage of the person-hours consumed by any major program. If what I wanted to do was to dream up new possibilities, I should stick to dreamy things like music and poetry, where talk is cheap and nearly sufficient.

Yet the truest form of the lesson might not have been so chastening after all. It would have sounded like pure arrogance at the time, even if I had had the temerity to formulate it: *This is no way to program computers.*

A decade or two later I could sit at my own computer, at my own desk, fiddling until my program worked. The real beginning of this approach came with the BASIC language, developed at Dartmouth specifically to teach people how to program. BASIC is an *interpreted* language. That means that you can type a statement on a keyboard, and the computer will respond directly by doing what your statement has told it to do. This is obviously good for learning. You can see your mistakes right away and correct them. But it requires that you have a computer at your immediate disposal. A batch-processed interpreted language would be an absurdity, like a car pulled by a team of goats or a game of Monopoly played by mail.

Historically, the first solution to the frozen bureaucracy surrounding computers was "time-sharing." This is a way of sharing the resources of a big computer among several people, all working at separate terminals that the central computer services in a round-robin. But time-sharing can slow down the computer's responses, and speed is the main virtue of a computer to begin with. Time-sharing just moves the bureaucracy inside the machine. The individual user's contact with the computer is still mediated by elaborate protocols (passwords, protected file systems, and so on). Ultimately, the way to implement a system of direct interaction between computers and the people who program and use them is to give every person her or his own computer.

That was the accomplishment of the late seventies and early eighties: the microcomputer revolution. Now everyone who can afford a good color TV *could* afford a small, usable computer. (This doesn't mean that everyone who's in a pinch will make that choice; but in 1995, sales of computers beat sales of TVs for the first time.) With the advent of the affordable desktop micro, the computer became exactly what I had thought it was until I got my final grade in the college course: a dreaming machine.

Interpreted languages like BASIC have some built-in limitations. They're often contrasted with *compiled* languages like FORTRAN and Pascal and C. In these, a special program called a compiler translates the code you write (which looks at least *somewhat* like a human language) into a code the machine can read. In the eighties very fast, cheap, powerful compilers came along and made this distinction less important. The feedback for the experimenter is pretty immediate either way. But in any case, all these developments have aimed in the same direction: toward placing as much computing power as possible in the hands of individual programmers, not reserving it for regimented initiates.

It's true that good computer programs that do complex and important tasks aren't usually written this way. They're written in many small pieces by large teams of highly trained, intelligent, cooperative people after a long period of planning. They aren't so much written as *conducted*, like military campaigns, and their success depends on the same virtues—plenty of resources (money, equipment, people), extreme care for details, and just the right bit of audacity.

But all over the world a growing number of people are *playing* with computers. And the most interesting play isn't like card or board games but like Erector sets.

If I were writing that chorale harmonization program now and put all my best fiddling into it, and it still wouldn't work, I would know I was up against one of three things: (a) a bit of fundamental ignorance about computers; (b) a bit of fundamental ignorance about the harmonization of chorales; or (c) a fundamental incompatibility between the computer and this project.

The first two problems would be interesting and informative. If I had the time to continue, I'd sit down and learn enough to rectify them. The third problem might be still more interesting. It would mean that I'd encountered something computers simply can't do. This third possibility brings me back to questions I was trying to explore in that college course.

I think now that I undertook my computer chorale project because I was fascinated by a certain kind of boundary. The year before, I had completed the rigorous introductory course for music majors. We had learned to harmonize chorales, even on sight (the final exam was terrifying). This is a peculiar skill and by no means a simple one, but its relation to musical composition was not very clear.

"Musical composition" was the name of that sphere of activity in which J. S. Bach excelled. Along the way toward that lofty sphere the ardent student spent a year learning the rules of harmony and voice-leading. It was the idea of a *gradus ad Parnassum*, an apprenticeship climb up the steep hill of the Muses. To anyone who had practiced and practiced playing an instrument, this concept of progressing from the technical elements to the real music seemed quite plausible. Yet there was also an obvious gap between exercises and music. It's not unlike the gap between mindless neurons and the mind they make up.

I do *not* mean that Bach's music was inexpressibly sublime and the rules were mere mechanical drudgery. I had learned enough in high school from my composer friend Charles Wolterink to see that the beauty of Bach's music was inseparable from the complex beauty of the tonal system he used (and helped perfect). The grandeur of many passages in his music depended on a sense of inevitability in the way the system worked out its own consequences. It's often compared to the grand beauty of mathematics, though Newtonian physics might supply a clearer analogy. The musical "rules" were the map or skeleton of that same system. They weren't petty restrictions, like parking laws, but possibilities of motion, like the rules of chess. Furthermore, the rules themselves, when you set them to work on a bit of musical material, could often produce some beautiful effects, as if automatically.

Bach, the master, usually abided by the same harmonic rules my teachers made me obey. So when it occurred to me that a computer could do what I had spent a year learning to do, that wasn't a reason to feel foolish or under mechanical attack. Instead, I became interested in formulating one part of musical knowledge by automating it. In part, it was a way of confirming what I knew and bringing it all into consciousness.

How was it that anyone could set out to compose impossibly beautiful music? First, learn the rules of harmony? Fine. Then counterpoint, then orchestration? Fine. If it could be done, it could be done in stages. But if it could be done in stages, and if these could be broken down and specified exactly enough, how far through the stages could a computer be taught to follow?

Sometimes Bach broke the rules. My favorite example was a passage near the end of the fifth fugue from the second book of the *Well-Tempered Clavier*—two measures in which the harmony suddenly goes completely berserk, unpredictable, barely analyzable. That wild moment couldn't be programmed, I was sure. But the beauty of Bach's music didn't depend on those rule-breaking moments. Rather, it had to do with some balance between rules and rulelessness. (It wasn't random, either. The boundaries among the random, the arbitrary, and the unpredictable will concern us later on.)

Though I didn't know it at the time, I was investigating something analogous to the question of "computability." Some problems (in mathematics, for instance) are computable, and others are not. To some questions, the answers can be determined in a finite amount of time; to others, not. (Marvin Minsky has written a hard but readable book on the theory of Finite Automata that treats this distinction in detail.) Researchers in artificial intelligence (AI, for short) are constantly wrestling with the question of whether aspects of human behavior ("intelligence" for short?) are computable or not. In a minor way, without much rigorous philosophical comprehension, I was puzzling over a similar kind of question. For me it was a matter of what was knowable about the process of musical composition; trying to compute it was a way of finding that out.

My main purpose in writing the chorale program wasn't to produce chorales, to save myself the labor of harmonizing them. The computer was a way of exploring the nature of what I knew about music. Later, when I began to use the computer in poetry, it would participate in a similar process of thought. Yet it would also turn out to *change* the poetry I would write, with or without a computer.

In the end I studied English; music became my avocation, not my profession. I wrote poems and published them. I studied poetry and wrote critical articles and books. I became a teacher of literature and of the writing of poetry. For a while, when I briefly tired of teaching, I worked as a technical writer for computer companies. Writing computer manuals is (at its most interesting, which is rare) an act of cultural translation: What your reader needs is to be initiated into a new way of thinking; your job is to lead the way across that border.

Poets tend to read widely, and as compared with other teachers we assign reading that sends students indiscriminately to all floors of the campus library. Literary critics who are interested in music or science or computers tend to wander away from traditionally defined regions of scholarly labor. Technical writers are amphibians between still different worlds. So much of what I did, during the years after college and graduate school, kept me thinking about the boundaries between different systems of knowledge, different specializations of mental activity, different ways of making things work.

My recent programming experiments have grown out of all this boundary crossing. Before I describe the experiments themselves, I need to skip across the biggest gap in the neighborhood. Let me try to describe some of what poetry looks like, at least to some poets, these days.

2

START WITH POETRY

Start with the idea of *juxtaposition*, which has come to be a fundamental principle of poetic structure. It's easiest to see at work in small, isolated examples, such as short Imagist poems from the first part of this century. Or here, at the climactic moment in a poem by Ezra Pound, translated from the Chinese as "The River-Merchant's Wife: A Letter":

> You dragged your feet when you went out.
> By the gate now, the moss is grown, the different mosses,
> Too deep to clear them away!
> The leaves fall early this autumn, in wind.
> The paired butterflies are already yellow with August
> Over the grass in the West garden;
> They hurt me. I grow older.

Here's another translation of the same lines, by Witter Bynner (who calls the poem "A Song of Ch'ang Kan"):

> Your footprints by our door, where I had watched you go,
> Were hidden, every one of them, under green moss,
> Hidden under moss too deep to sweep away.
> And the first autumn wind added fallen leaves.
> And now, in the Eighth-month, yellowing butterflies
> Hover, two by two, in our west-garden grasses. . . .
> And, because of all this, my heart is breaking
> And I fear for my bright cheeks, lest they fade.

What's striking about Pound's version is the jumps. The details are juxtaposed—placed side by side without transitions. He doesn't explain what the moss, the leaves, the butterflies, and August have to do with each other or what any of them have to do with the woman speaking in this "letter" to her husband, the "river-merchant."

In contrast, Bynner is very anxious to cover up the gaps. Look at all those *ands*. He takes great pains to tell us every point where we are and how we got there. "And now," for instance, is a signal to tell us that the woman is through talking about the past and therefore that the poem has reached a turning point. "Because of all this" instructs us to review everything that's come before. It's meant to prepare us for the emotional climax.

It does seem useful to keep readers informed about where they are. (It's certainly a primary rule of technical writing.) How does Pound get away without all those signposts that Bynner is so careful to provide for us?

Pound solves the first problem—making the switch into the present—by the simple expedient of switching to present-tense verbs. In other words, he uses a signal built into the structure of the English language to replace Bynner's awkwardly explicit transition. In comparison, how much does "and" really mean in Bynner's lines?

Bynner's "Because of all this" seems like a more substantial, expedient gesture of connection. Yet Pound reduces Bynner's last two lines to just six words: "They hurt me. I grow older."

Why does this work? It works because we readers deduce. (Think of all we deduce from Pound's title.) In reading this terse line we begin (without thinking about it) by identifying "they" as the butterflies. To understand how the butterflies can "hurt me," we have to recall that they are paired and the speaker isn't, which in turn evokes the whole history of the marriage that earlier stanzas have told. So Pound finds a way to make his readers do automatically what Bynner insists on waving a big flag about.

Because Pound doesn't supply the connections, we do. That's the basic idea. Through juxtaposition the poet lets the structure of the language do the work of a lot of explanation. And in the process the poet enlists the reader's help in making the connections that make meaning. Enlisted, we become engaged.

Pound, T. S. Eliot, and William Carlos Williams all discovered important variations on the principle of juxtaposition. Local effects like the ones we've just seen were only the beginning. These poets went on to use juxtaposition in building new kinds of long poems: Pound in the *Cantos*, Eliot in *The Waste Land* and *Four Quartets*, and Williams in *Paterson*. In these big works, the most influential poems in the first half of this century, they set whole sections next to each other without transition. The sections often differ strikingly in subject, voice, and form. The links of narrative, history, and logical implication that hold the poem together are left for us to supply, guided by the arrangement of the pieces. The coherence of the poem and, finally, its activity of meaning reside in these gaps the poet leaves in the structure. In Beethoven the silences are no less important than the notes; in Modernist poetry the juxtapositions say as much as do the lines themselves.

In fact, juxtaposition became a kind of trademark, a defining characteristic of Modernism in poetry, beginning before World War I and continuing into the present. Yet the principle is older than that. Poets since before Homer have valued the special kind of eloquence that comes from silence. We're all good enough rhetoricians to know that reticence and understatement can be more powerful than exaggeration.

John Lennon and Paul McCartney probably learned this trick from the old ballads that are every English-speaking person's poetic heritage. Think of the final verse of "And I Love Her," which juxtaposes bright stars and dark sky with undying love. Logically, what do these astronomical commonplaces have to do with the declaration of eternal love? Yet the conviction we hear in the song comes partly from the juxtaposition between an obvious universal truth and what might, all by itself, be a more dubious human affirmation. Any attempt to make an explicit transition would just turn it into a lie.

Again, it's we who supply the sense of conviction. The poet seems to do nothing but state the facts. Juxtaposition makes the reader an accomplice in the poem, forging the links of meaning. In the process we supply a lot of energy, and that involves us in the poem.

It follows that the bigger the gap, the more powerful the effect (as long as we can cross it at all). Metaphor works the same way. If the two things a metaphor compares are very close to each other to begin with, the metaphor doesn't do very much. "This car's a pile of junk" is emphatic but not revelatory. If they're more different, the metaphor seems to release a larger amount of meaning. When Marvell speaks of oranges on the tree as "golden lamps in a green night," the echoes resound in the chasm we've had to leap.

Eventually, though, the gap would get to be too big to cross. What happens then? When we can't make the leap, we call what we're reading *nonsense*. It doesn't make sense, or more accurately, we no longer know how to make sense of it.

In this context, the term "nonsense verse" is something of a misnomer. Lewis Carroll's poems work, not by failing to make sense but by teasing our ability to make sense of them. Some, like "Jabberwocky," depend simply on made-up words:

> 'Twas brillig, and the slithy toves
> Did gyre and gimble in the wabe . . .

We don't know what "brillig" means or "slithy toves" or "wabe." Yet we can guess a lot quite easily. "Toves" have to be animals of some kind (the movements that "gyre and gimble" connote are too active for plants waving in the breeze). "Brillig" has to be a season or weather, and a "wabe" an item of landscape or time of day. The syntactical system of English, which Carroll leaves intact while disrupting the vocabulary, carries a far greater proportion of the meaning of a sentence than we're usually aware of.

(Actually, many of the apparently new words in "Jabberwocky" turn out to be archaic or obscure words that Carroll, knowingly or not, partially redefined. "Gyre" means "spiral"; gimbals, sometimes spelled "gimbles," are pivots on which things like lamps swing back and forth. Often the original meaning seems to have at least some influence on his invented usage. The inertia of a language system is really enormous.)

Other poems from the Alice books disorient our reading more

subtly. The "paper of verses" read by the White Rabbit in evidence against the Knave is full of stanzas like this:

> I gave her one, they gave him two,
>   You gave us three or more;
> They all returned from him to you,
>   Though they were mine before.

Some kind of "plot" is still clear here. The consecutive numbers contribute. So do cues like "though" and "before." And there's a constant movement *away*, toward the third-person him and them, and *returning* to you and me. If it weren't for these continuities, the poem wouldn't be just "nonsense"; it would be gibberish and uninteresting. Carroll simply obscures his language's *reference* to anything in the familiar world by the disorder he lets loose among the pronouns.

"Serious" poets disrupt the ordinary patterns of meaning, too, sometimes in ways that strikingly resemble Carrollian "nonsense." Here's the beginning of John Ashbery's "The Grapevine" (from his 1956 book, *Some Trees*):

> Of who we and all they are
> You all now know. But you know
> After they began to find us out we grew
> Before they died thinking us the causes
> Of their acts.

Like Carroll, in this and many other poems, Ashbery obscures his references to the nonlinguistic world we think we all know in common. Yet the sense of the language, its internal relations of syntax and semantic categories, remains largely intact. Again "they" are ranged against "we" and "you." And words like "know," and "find out," and "thinking" suggest a train of thought.

The result, as Alice says of "Jabberwocky," is that "it seems to fill my head with ideas—only I don't know exactly what they are." So this kind of language is a little like music, which refers to nothing but which no one would call meaningless. And it's clear why poets need to do this. Our daily use of language is made possible by habits and conventions, but habit makes our language boring and dead. Humpty Dumpty says the question about words is "which is to be master—that's all." As a critic, Roger Holmes, remarked, "In one sense words are our masters, or communication would be impossible. In another we are the masters; otherwise there could be no poetry." Language working on autopilot lets us talk our way through our days. But the aerobatics that teach us what the craft can do require an alert hand on the controls.

Understanding isn't additive. Meaning doesn't accumulate word by word as we trudge through a sentence. It precipitates, as rain precipitates out of air under the right conditions. (In the recent language of Complexity Theory, meaning is an *emergent phenomenon*.) Reading takes place within a context, and the context is present at the reading because the reader brings it along. We readers are always helping supply meaning, which suggests that juxtaposition is at work in all acts of sense making. Sense is never absolutely continuous; there are irreducible gaps. (Bynner's anxious *ands* were futile from the start.) Poetry tends to make us more aware of the gaps than does conversation or political speeches. Some poets emphasize the gaps among single words, as in the "Jabberwocky" style of nonsense. Others emphasize the gulf that separates one whole sentence from the next. Most poetry stays between these extremes, surprising us most frequently on the level of the phrase and the line.

Take Laura Jensen, a strange and exemplary poet, whose sixth book, *Memory*, was published in 1982. It contains a wonderful spooky poem about a cat, called "The Clean One." Jensen begins with the animal's pretty fastidiousness—

> He gathers them close, the pads of his paws,
> Like a nosegay of kisses.

—and ends with the violence of its predation:

> But instead, in his teeth he carries
> the bird to some private corner,
> slits the breast with his claw, a razor,
> and the light of the heart spills into time.

Looking just at three lines, the first two and the last, let's see what a dance the reader does at the poem's instigation.

In a way, everything seems simple enough in the first line. It's easy to visualize the cat flexing its paws as cats do. The next line adds a simile, which shouldn't be a problem. But actually we take some bigger steps than we expect, like missing one stair on the way down. The paws resemble a nosegay, a bouquet of flowers. Yet paws are more like hands holding a bouquet than the bouquet itself; two things have gotten blended. And it's a nosegay not of flowers but of kisses. So there's a metaphor (kisses for flowers) within the simile (paws like a nosegay). The echo between "nose" and "kisses" may evoke the cat washing its face, justifying the name, "the Clean One." Furthermore, if what the cat gathers the paws close to is his mouth, then the "kisses" seem not just three steps removed from the beginning but also a return to the beginning.

The kind of attention we're called on to pay here makes us notice that the first line, too, was a bit peculiar after all. "The pads of his paws" now seems an odd phrase, as if the pads and paws could be detached from each other. The nosegay is suddenly exploded into separate flowers. It's often this way: Strangeness radiates from certain areas of a poem and suffuses the language of the whole thing—and sometimes, for a while, our feeling for language outside the poem.

In the final line, "the light of the heart" has a different kind of density. It might be a phrase describing something abstract, like true understanding—"enlightenment," we say. But also when the cat "slits the breast" of the bird, exposing the heart, he literally brings light to the heart, which is also death. Hearts need to do their work in the dark. At the same time, the verb "spills" makes the "light" the heart's blood. And while the blood spills "into time," into mortality and decay, this exiles the heart's owner, the bird, out of time into death. Reading a line like this, we're aware of how much is being brought together; but that depends on things being split apart by our sharpened attention.

Jensen's work capitalizes on technical discoveries—discoveries about uses of language—that have been made by a couple of generations of modern poets. Some contemporary poetry goes still farther in pursuing the attention to gaps in sense and the complicity between poets and readers in the making of meaning. In the last couple of decades, some poets have pursued these insights into language, not just as a poetic method but as the content or subject of their poems.

Barrett Watten's "Complete Thought" is built from fifty pairs of sentences. The poem's topic is the relation between these pairs, and often their topic is themselves. Here's XVI:

> I am speaking in an abridged form.
> Ordinary voices speak in rooms.

We can't read this without thinking in an unaccustomed way about the treacherous depths of the little word "in." And do the two sentences, juxtaposed, imply an equation between "I" and a "voice"?

In Rosmarie Waldrop's haunting line, "The proportion of accident in my picture of the world falls with the rain," we can hardly tell where we stumbled. On "with"? Back on "falls"? Or only at "rain"? Or did we not miss any turning at all—in which case, why does the sentence feel so odd, and does all language potentially feel just as unstable? (In this book, *The Reproduction of Profiles* [New Directions, 1987], Waldrop is also splicing and revising phrases from the language philosopher Wittgenstein, which adds still more disorienting echoes.)

Ron Silliman (whose book of essays called *The New Sentence* offers the best explanations of this kind of poetry) has a thirty-page prose poem called "Sunset Debris" (in *The Age of Huts*) made entirely of questions, ranging all the way from "Ain't it a bitch?" to "Why is it that painters now are so obsessed with the elimination of space, that composers want to obliterate time, that writers feel compelled to remove the referential?" This massive consistency shifts our attention to the nature of questions themselves. Each sentence, rather than asking something (like questions in conversation) begins to *exemplify questioning*.

This shift resembles the distinction that linguists make between *use* and *mention*. If I say, "The vixens protect their dens," I'm *using* the word "vixens" to talk about female foxes. If I say, " 'Vixens' is a great Scrabble word," I'm *mentioning* the word "vixens." One effect of poetry can be to shift its language from use toward mention, making us aware of words and sentences partly *as* language and not simply as references to nonlinguistic things. This need not be trivial or a retreat from human concerns. Much of the mystery in our relation to the world is embodied in language's mysterious relation.

Again, the movement of poems like these resembles the movement that gives meaning to music. The unfolding of one phrase into the next, the rise and fall of sound and feeling, the shifts and contrasts, mean something in themselves, beyond the propositions the poem offers about the world. But if poetry is like music, music is also like mathematics. And again Lewis Carroll, a mathematical logician whose poetry and fiction were hobbies, showed the way toward the poetry of logic.

In the long Romantic period—perhaps not over yet—poetic truth and logical truth often seemed opposed. (So did science and literature, the "two cultures." So would computers and poetry.) Looking back at Lewis Carroll's work in the middle of the nineteenth century, though, we begin to see the potential similarity of logical and poetic structures. His exercises in symbolic logic lead up to surrealistic conclusions like "No hedge-hog takes in the *Times*." Here's the set of propositions he uses to prove that "I always avoid a kangaroo."

 1. The only animals in this house are cats;
 2. Every animal is suitable for a pet, that loves to gaze at the moon;
 3. When I detest an animal, I avoid it;
 4. No animals are carnivorous, unless they prowl at night;
 5. No cat fails to kill mice;
 6. No animals ever take to me, except what are in this house;
 7. Kangaroos are not suitable for pets;
 8. None but carnivora kill mice;
 9. I detest animals that do not take to me;
10. Animals, that prowl at night, always love to gaze at the moon.

The temptation to read these sentences as a poem is strong. Just so, a poem by David Antin called "Stanzas" is made up entirely of the artificial logical structures we call syllogisms. They begin simply enough:

> if the street is sprinkled there is no dust in the air
> the street is sprinkled
> there is no dust in the air

But by the second page we're getting this:

> pillows are soft
> pokers are not
> pillows are not pokers

True, and logically valid—but somehow all wrong. We don't tell pillows from pokers by syllogistic reasoning. This mode of argument seems bizarre when it bumps against our real world. And it isn't just logic that's threatened:

> if war is declared the country will be invaded
> war is not declared
> the country is invaded

This doesn't follow. We know that some logic has been violated. Later, when we read

> if war is declared the country will be invaded
> war is declared
> the country is invaded

we know that (1) the logic is correct and (2) the conclusion may be true, but (3) there's no connection between the two. The conclusion follows from historical necessities on which formal logic has no realistic grip. By the end of Antin's poem, he can show how this gap admits incredible (but chillingly familiar) reasoning like this:

> all Germans are white men
> all civilized men are white
> all Germans are civilized

Syllogisms pretend to be impersonal language—the objective voice of truth. But any real use of language resounds with voices that aren't impersonal or objective at all. Antin's poem sets the language of logic (the syllogistic form) against the logic of language (the content determined by personal and historical circumstances). The struggle between these two voices and among all the voices that inevitably resound in his language is the meaning of the poem. It's a political meaning; political interactions are linguistic.

Poets working in this area are often called, reasonably enough, "language" poets. Many of them are interested in linguistics. Before this century, linguists mostly studied phonetics and the origins of words. Modern linguistics begins with Ferdinand de Saussure's idea of language as a "structure of differences." Saussure's approach has turned out to be a useful way to think about at least some poetry.

Language is a "structure of differences" in the sense that words don't get their meaning directly from referring to things in the world. They get their meaning from their relations to other words, most basically from their distinctions. Phonetically, *cat* is different from *bat* because of the difference between the sounds *c* and *b*. If it weren't for that difference, the two words couldn't refer to different animals. So the words are defined in the first place by their places within a self-contained system of language. Many words have meaning only because of their relations within that system: *which*, *the*, *only*, and so on.

This idea sometimes puzzles people. How can a self-contained system mean anything? This turns out to be similar to another puzzle: How can computers store and manipulate information? From a logical standpoint, a computer is just a box full of switches. Each switch is either on or off. We can call *on* 1 and *off* 0, though that's just a convention. (It's also a convention to call each 1-or-0 switch a "bit" of information, for "binary digit.") Inside the box, *on* is a certain electrical voltage, and *off* is a different voltage. How can two levels of voltage, or even 1's and 0's, refer to anything outside the box, such as planes approaching an airport?

If you ask a computer what it's thinking, in its own terms, the answer will be 11010001011110101101101010100101. . . . There has to be a prearranged code to translate this into our terms (and vice versa, of course). One popular code says that the pattern 01000001 will stand for a capital *A*, 00101011 for a plus sign, and so on. There are 128 of these "ASCII code" equivalences. Another code, known to the CPU (the central processing unit) and used for calculation rather than data, says that 01000110 will stand for the instruction "add one to the number found at such-and-such a place in memory." The computer knows which code to apply from the context.

What does this have to do with poetry?

Maybe nothing. Maybe it's just a suggestive analogy, and maybe only my own quirk makes it even that. But there's a common thread running through everything we've looked at in these preliminary chapters. How do grand structures of meaning get built up out of bits and pieces? Chorales and constitutions and cathedrals are products of human thought, which seems to be the product of brain cells, but the path from one end of this chain to the other is remarkably devious. Poetry is one way of exploring the maze of mind. It's time to go back and retrace how I came to use computers in that exploration.

3

THE SINCLAIR ZX81

The first computer I ever owned was a Sinclair ZX81. It was a pretty remarkable machine. If you built it yourself, it cost $49.95; in 1981 a "serious" computer might cost a hundred times that. It had one kilobyte of memory. That means that it could deal with about half a page of data at any one time, or a few hundred computer instructions, or a little bit of each. Desktop computers now hold thousands of times as much. External data storage was on a painfully slow cassette tape; the keyboard was a membrane about the right size for a two-year-old; its output was a fuzzy picture on a television set. Yet the CPU (the calculating heart of the computer) was the powerful Z80 chip, and the clever use of specially designed circuits called gate arrays allowed for a decent built-in BASIC language.

The directions for assembling the ZX81 were good and clear as far as they went, but it was a long afternoon I spent putting mine together. After several hours I figured out the main trouble. The instructions had omitted any step that connected the power supply to the computing circuits themselves. I picked a plausible spot to join them and for the hundredth time tried plugging the machine in. The screen of my old Heathkit black-and-white TV (another gadget I'd built) was still full of snow. I fiddled with dials and wires, trying to get the little white-on-black letter K (the ZX81's cursor) to appear. Quite suddenly what did show up was the beatific Mr. Rogers, crouched down behind his fish tank, wearing a skin diver's mask, and talking in a dreamy voice about all the colors of the fish, which to me looked gray on gray.

Eventually the computer worked as advertised. Besides the built-in BASIC, you could use low-level assembly-language programming to fit somewhat larger programs into that nutshell of memory. Still, nothing very elaborate was going to come out of the Sinclair. It was a learning computer. And of course it was all mine; it was the first computer I could learn inside out.

One of the last programs I wrote on the ZX81, before I replaced it with a much roomier IBM PC, was a poetry composer. I choose the term with some care. In keeping with the idea of juxtaposition, modern poets sometimes talk about the poem not as a process or speech so much as a composition. Poets who do so are usually thinking in terms of an analogy with the visual arts. The artist's job is to *compose*, to place together in a meaningful arrangement a number of independent elements. Painters compose planes of color, shapes, collaged objects, and so on. The poet's equivalents might be words, lines, phrases, quotations—any pieces of speech that can be treated as separable and rearranged in some poetic "space."

What my poetry composer arranged was lines; the BASIC program was called RanLines. It let you type in twenty short lines, which it stored in an internal array. Then, each time you pressed a key, the computer chose one of the lines at random and printed it on the screen. This is about the simplest possible kind of "computer poem." Yet even this beginning exercise raises a couple of points that remain important in far more sophisticated programs.

One of the Greek oracles, the sibyl at Cumae, used to write the separate words of her prophecies on leaves and then fling them out of the mouth of her cave. It was up to the suppliants to gather the leaves and make what order they could. The products of my first experiment were a little like that:

> THE RAMIFYING SUNLIGHT
> FOR A NEW NAME AND ADDRESS
> DEMANDS MINOR DISCRETIONS
> BIRCH BRANCHES
> OF A PIECE WITH THE LONG HAUL AND THE TREADMILL
> PRETENSE OF URGENCY
> KEEPING BEHIND IT ALL, ON TOP OF THE WORLD

AND THE TREE IS LILACS

AND THE TREE IS LILACS

WHATEVER YOUR PLANS, THE AFTERNOON
DEMANDS MINOR DISCRETIONS
THE OVERPLUS OF PLENTY
BIRCH BRANCHES
KEEPING BEHIND IT ALL, ON TOP OF THE WORLD

What the ZX81 program contributed to the act of writing poetry was a simple sort of randomness. This has always been the main contribution that computers have made to the writing of poetry. A little book called Energy Crisis Poems, published in 1974 in "an addition of 500 copies" with the subtitle "poetry by program / program by rjs," appears to have been generated in a similar way, as the introduction explains:

> the order of the lines within the poems was selected at random by the program from the input through an explosion of the least significant bits of the interval timer, which is updated every 26.04166 microseconds. The odds against an identical set of poems being created using the same input & parameters are approximately 5919247325225209600000000000000000-000000 to 1 . . .

What the "input" was, the explanatory note doesn't say. But my guess is that the program, like its predecessor the Auto-Beatnik, was given some syntactical templates—
[nouns] of [adjective] [noun]
[verb] [adverb]
from [adjective] [noun] to [adjective] [noun]

—together with some lists of words and perhaps phrases. The computer would then choose among these lists of parts at random, and each random collection that appealed to the programmer's aesthetic sense would go into the book:

> compoundings of senile enlightenment
> flagellate emptily
> from elemental origins to computer complexities . . .

these frayed lines you see bending
elastically whip and snap
in this ecstatically splintered womb

The principle is the same one used by Steve Allen in the old "Mad Libs" game.

Other early computer poetry reads much like this and feels as though it was produced in the same way. Haiku were especially common. The reasons are clear from the history of modern Imagist poetry. As both poets and programmers have realized, for different reasons, the reader's mind works most actively on sparse materials. We draw the clearest constellations from the fewest stars. So the nonsense factor is low for a tiny collocation of words that can be imbued with imagistic significance. It's hard to put together two words that don't make some kind of sense to the willing reader. If the language goes on longer, we begin to expect more discursive sense, and we more quickly grow suspicious of randomness.

My Sinclair ZX8 1 version of a poetry composer gave the computer an especially simple version of the random-language task, as befit an especially simple computer. I didn't ask it to fill in any blanks or to make choices on more than one linguistic level (both words and phrases, say). None of its choices depended on other choices. All it did, moment after moment, was to reach into its little bag of lines and pull one out. If it pulled out the one built-in blank line, there was a stanza break— at random. It would often repeat lines, as in the sample output given earlier. It had no memory of what it had just done. It could have no sense of structure in what it was putting together. To put it another way, the program could produce a simplistic kind of poetry forever, but it could never, by itself, produce a poem. All sense of completeness, progress, or implication was strictly a reader's ingenious doing.

Well, not strictly. A clever choice of lines for the input could help. The more discrete and self-contained the syntax of the line (complete clause, complete prepositional phrase), the more easily it joins with lines before and after. Keeping verb tense the same increases the opportunities for coherence. Short sharp images stand alone better than bits of narrative or argument.

The lines used for the sample I gave before favor variety and disjunction. A different store of lines could favor continuity instead. But continuity isn't closure. Only the act of a person, deciding to stop the program, establishes a defining boundary for the poem. The decision to stop (and maybe to select, to edit the output) can be completely arbitrary. The user can decide beforehand to produce exactly fourteen lines or can respond intuitively to the computer's output as it appears. But a human decision, though its motivation may be unknowably complex or obscure, can't be random.

The very simplicity of the program shows especially clearly the fundamental mystery of randomness in the writing of poetry. This is a thread running through all computer poetry, and it's worth examining in more detail.

There are other methods besides computers for introducing randomness into compositional processes. John Cage was a pioneer in the use of dice and other aleatory, or chance, procedures in music composition. Quite a while ago, Jackson Mac Low followed Cage's lead, beginning with music but soon turning back to his own art of poetry. Both men have been practicing Zen Buddhists, though neither seems very interested in what Mac Low calls the "spooky" aspects of Zen. Still, as Buddhists they see the workings of the universe in ways that diverge from the Cartesisan deterministic tradition of Western science.

For determinists, anything random is mere noise, just crud gumming up the clean machine of the universe. But the non-Aristotelian logic of Buddhism (and many other cultural traditions) finds a different place for accident. To someone who believes that the universe is thoroughly coherent and that human action is consistent with that coherence, dice fall the way they must at any particular moment.

Different views of propositional logic entail different ideas about causality. From one scientific perspective, the idea of meaningful coincidence is simply superstition:

1. We threw those virgins into the volcano
2. It stopped erupting
3. We'll act more promptly next time.

(I owe the example to my colleague Julia Genster.) The fact that this fallacy has a Latin name—*post hoc, ergo propter hoc*—shows that we've recognized it for a long time. In contrast, Carl Jung (a Western psychological scientist with Eastern proclivities) proposed the concept of *synchronicity*: that events occurring at the same time are fundamentally connected, and examining one of them can lead to insights about the other. Jung wrote the preface for a famous edition of the I Ching, the Chinese book of divination that depends on this kind of faith in the order of things. Casting one particular hexagram at one particular time reveals a truth about that moment.

When two events occurring at the same time are one person's mental events, there's not much doubt that they're connected. In thought there are no accidents. "Random thoughts" are always linked by unconscious motivations. Freud (Jung's mentor but certainly never as radical a critic of determinism) declared that there are no accidents in *any* aspect of our behavior, including actions we disown, including things that simply "happen" to us. That's why there can be a "psychopathology of everyday life" and a psychoanalytic interpretation of dreams, which an earlier science would have written off as witchcraft.

"Happen" comes from a word that means "chance." The idea of synchronicity (and even the Freudian idea of unconscious motivaton) can be seen in two ways. Either nothing occurs at random, or random events are themselves meaningful. It's the latter idea—acknowledging randomness and finding meaning in it—that strikes many Western people as strange, irresponsible, and even frightening.

But for thousands of years people have been consulting chance for advice: throwing the I Ching, inspecting birds' entrails, opening the *Aeneid* or the Bible at random, and so on. However severely modern science condemns this as sloppy thinking, it has at least a firm old lineage.

And it turns out that science isn't so single-minded about all this. Einstein wanted to think it was: "I shall never believe that God plays dice with the world." But by rejecting the randomness at the heart of quantum mechanics, Einstein, who set the course of twentieth-century physics, cut himself off from its progress. Subatomic particles behave in ways that are radically indeterminate and unpredictable, random not just incidentally but in principle. That, the physicists now assure us, is how the world really is.

Attuning themselves to how the world really is, is an old ambition of poets. Our earliest function was to keep the local gods happy by praising them. (It remains our most natural service, I think.) Though the alliance between prophecy and poetry isn't always to the advantage of either, it goes a long way back. And if the religion is Druidism or Buddhism or Quantum Mechanical Scientism, randomness becomes a plausible religious rite and a reasonable method for poetry.

Not many contemporary poets feel comfortable with such a grand reading of their role in the universe. And in any case, this is all off-duty theorizing. What a poet worries about while writing poems is likely to be more practical. At its baldest, the poet's problem is to write poems that will engage the attention of readers.

(A footnote here: What a poet's really conscious of while writing a poem, most of us will insist, is the poem itself, not the audience. The question is complicated, because the mind is always shifting in toward the heart of the poem and out toward the world it grows from and will grow back into. But the fact remains that few poets can keep going for very long on poems they don't think *anyone* will read.)

Poems are partly incubated in the warm matrix of tradition. Poets and readers share a half-tacit knowledge of this background. It supplies a context for the experience of poetry and a basis for communication. But this is a problem as well as a support. The same background of literary history that helps a reader to recognize a poem *as* a poem threatens to determine so much about it that it becomes boringly predictable. As Howard Nemerov puts it, "The poet's task has generally been conceded to be hard, but it may be so described as to make it logically impossible: Make an object recognizable as an individual of the class *p* for poem, but make it in such a way that it resembles no other individual of that class."

So a more direct use of randomness is to *reduce the level of probability* in the poems. If the next word in the line I'm writing comes at random, I can at least be sure that it won't be coming from a cliché.

Part of my hope is to surprise the reader; part of it is to surprise myself. The idea isn't just to make the process of writing more entertaining but to *authenticate* it. If I'm discovering, the reader is more likely to have a sense of discovery. Again, the problem is compounded by history. From our reading and our classrooms we learn classical canons of taste and value. When we're writing more or less classically constructed poems — and most poets still do, at least during a period of apprenticeship — these canons continue to operate more or less well. They tell us what we're doing, what it fits into, what comes next, and what it's worth. But these canons fall silent during our work on other kinds of poems. How do we know whether a given word, line, sentence is the *right* one to add to the poem when the poem is breaking new ground? If it really is "given," or "inspired" as we used to say, how do we know whether to trust the source of it? How do we tell false from true inspiration, dreams through the ivory gate from dreams through the gate of horn?

Then we're flying by the seat of the pants. This also makes revision difficult — not difficult in the old sense of being hard work but difficult to justify, point by point. That's one reason a lot of poets, following the lead of the jazz musicians, have become interested in improvisation. The improvisor can't edit but must fall back on the most basic standard of all: Is this interesting to me, right now? And this implies the hope that I can be, as well as the writer, a good enough representative of the reader to judge for both of us.

If I can't surprise myself, it's very difficult to interest myself (though of course, surprise doesn't guarantee interest). Furthermore, if I can be surprised, that ensures my closer alliance with the reader I'm standing in for. If using randomness makes me a little more passive — a little more obviously a judge than a creator — that's another similarity between me and the reader and another point of contact for the poem. I allow myself to be not perfectly in control.

None of this deliberation about strategy really explains the fascination of programs like the little one running on my ZX81. It doesn't account for the fact that I could fascinatedly watch the program produce a number of "poems" this way but never seriously consider adopting the program as my customary method of writing poems. Other poets who saw the machine's little trick seemed fascinated as well, but none of them ran out to buy computers as a result. Simple randomness won't suffice to shock language into poetry, though chance will play an important part in experiments we'll see later.

In the meantime, a more atavistic pleasure such programs give is that of delegating a human function to something else. We tell ourselves many stories about this: stories of the golem, of Frankenstein's monster, of robots, automatons, and so on. Through these machines we place ourselves in the role of creators as well as creatures.

But this secondary creation tends to make writers (and other "creative" people) nervous. Your self gets tied up in what you make. A computer that becomes too autonomous begins to feel like a usurper. Just who's in charge here after all? For instance, even this first simple program raised questions about *authorship*. Exactly who wrote the poem I presented earlier? Me? The computer? The program? Myself through the computer?

The title page of *Energy Crisis Poems* proclaims that "anyone with access to an IBM S360 or S370 running under OS or OS/VS can use the program exactly as it exists." We might hear a hint of participatory democracy left over (in 1974) from the sixties. The hint recurs in my fifty-dollar Sinclair computer. A touch of radical democracy, even of anarchy, is implicit in today's ubiquitous desktop computers. True, the proliferation threatens new ways of regimenting workers, and so on. But potentially, the microcomputer revolution of the late seventies extended the social revolutions of the previous decade. (That was hardly the manufacturers' main motive. But it was important to some of the designers, many of whom were hackers with a subversive bent.) In this atmosphere we might expect the privilege and heirophany associated with Authorship and Authority to come under scrutiny. For Buddhists like John Cage and Jackson Mac Low, that curtailment of the ego's realm amounts to a liberation.

These questions come up in more interesting forms as later programs mediate in more complex ways between the programmer/poet and the final result. In the meantime, my story turns to quite a different use of the computer, a program with a quite different intellectual pedigree.

>>>> **/ 4 /**

THE SCANSION MACHINE

A search of the catalog in a big library turns up quite a few cross-references between "computers" and "poetry." But virtually all of the books and articles referred to have to do with "computer stylistics." That is, they're documents in the field of literary criticism, and they represent endeavors to *study* poetry by means of computers, not experiments in *making* poetry with computers.

Computers are well suited to some tasks that are useful to certain kinds of literary criticism. In my college computer class, one project the teacher suggested was a dictionary program that would organize a list of words so that a particular one could be retrieved quickly. The methods involved—searching and sorting—are the bread and butter of computer science and have been exhaustively researched. These are computer capabilities just there for the asking. If the study of literature can use them, it's welcome.

And it can. The classic literary computer project is the concordance: a list of all the words that appear in a certain work (or all the works by a certain author or, in the grandest concordance so far, the *Thesaurus Linguae Graecae*, the whole of classical Greek literature). The list is arranged in alphabetical order for easy reference, preferably with an indication of the context for each appearance of the word. Concordances used to be prepared painfully by hand, usually by many hands. In the precomputer age, therefore, they existed only for a small number of very important books: the Bible, Shakespeare, the complete works of a handful of poets.

Nowadays creating a concordance is vastly easier. The methods for converting the text into a list of entries and arranging these in accessible order are well understood. Programs for doing these things circulate more or less freely in the academic publishing community. The job can even be done on a home computer, though the first and last stages are tedious. Before the computer can break down and sort the original text, someone has to put it into machine-readable form. This remains a large, labor-intensive effort. A book long enough to be worth a concordance would take days or weeks for one person to type in, and perhaps months to check for accuracy. Automatic text scanners can mechanize the big job of input, but even good OCR (optical character recognition) programs, which can read a wide variety of typefaces and deal with defective printing, still need scrupulous proofreading. (Many advertise 99 percent accuracy, but that's a couple of dozen errors per page.) And once the concordance is made, publishing the finished book isn't a family-room job. (Actually, concordances are less and less often printed as books at all but "published" over computer networks.)

Aside from helping you find a passage you half-remember, a concordance can be informative. If you want to know what the Bible means by the word *covenant*, a good first step would be to read all 481 passages that use it. For this reason, I wrote an *interactive* concordance generator. It shows you a text (that you've put "on-line") and lets you browse, choosing particular words to "concord," which it can do very quickly. Each instance of the word or phrase appears in the middle of a line of context—a KWIC, or Key-Word In Context concordance. You can sort these lines in many ways to see what words follow or precede the one concorded. This kind of study of a long poem, for instance, can reveal unsuspected patterns. If *and* almost always follows a comma, the poet favors compound sentences more than compound phrases. If *be* ends many sentences, the poem is bound to feel "philosophical."

Furthermore, the kind of information found in a full concordance can be generalized into a kind of statistical characterization of an author's style. (Hence, the term computer stylistics.) How large is his or her vocabulary? How specialized? What's the ratio of active to passive verbs? How often does she or he turn nouns into adjectives?

What proportion of the verbs are modified by adverbs? This kind of authorial profile can sometimes help to identify the author of a doubtful work or straighten out the chronology of an author's writings.

I've never found this species of scholarship the most interesting kind of literary criticism to do, though I'm glad to benefit from its results. It does appeal to some part of me—just as sometimes, when an important problem is bubbling on the back burner, I enjoy making indexes of my music collection. Order and information have their own appeal, beyond usefulness. Computers offer endless opportunities for this kind of fiddling. Like most laborsaving devices, they create as much work as they perform. (So are fears about automation destroying jobs groundless in the long run? Well, it's in the short run that people need to eat.)

But beyond such distractions, statistical analysis may provide insights that again have to do with the boundary between the mechanical and the creative. Counting verbs, for instance, is mechanical. But discovering that Shakespeare activates his language by making new verbs out of nouns is a creative act of reading. No simple sum of mechanical acts will automatically generate the discovery, yet the counting is a path toward the discovery. Furthermore, counting (if it's done with intelligence and imagination) can be used to prove a more general thesis than a single flash of intuition. Walter Jackson Bate, in his biography of Samuel Johnson, pursues the clue of a very high percentage of active verbs in Johnson's poetry toward a comprehensive picture of Johnson's surprisingly powerful use of abstract language.

Stylistics is not my field. But one of my fields has been prosody: the study of poetic meter and rhythms. So one of the first large computer projects I undertook was a Scansion Machine.

Scansion means marking the way a line of metrical verse uses its underlying meter. The meter is an unchanging abstraction; but any particular line realizes and varies the pattern, and that produces the rhythmic interest of metrical poetry. Scansion helps show the relation between general meter and particular rhythm.

There are two main ways to scan verse these days. There's the traditional method, like this:

x / | x / | x / | x / | x /

The curfew tolls the knell of parting day

It sees the line as a series of *feet*, conventional rhythmic groupings of stressed and unstressed syllables. There's also a newer method, originated by Morris Halle and Samuel J. Keyser, based on generative linguistics. From their general study of stress in English words and phrases, Halle and Keyser derive formulas that determine whether a line is metrical or unmetrical.

For the Scansion Machine, I chose the older method for several reasons. First, it requires a bit less lexical information—less elaborate cataloging of how individual words are formed and pronounced. Therefore, it's less "data-intensive" and more "computation-intensive." The important task in traditional scansion is figuring out how the line is made up of its constituent units, or feet (iambs, trochees, etc.), rather than compiling a lot of data about particular words. But both methods require some lexical data, and this difference between them is small.

Second, I wasn't convinced that the newer method has as much to do with how people actually read poetry. Meter is a body of conventions, a set of mutual understandings between the poet and the reader, more than a matter of unconscious linguistic knowledge (like syntax). In this sense, the very fact that traditional scansion is traditional gives it an advantage of accuracy.

Third, while the new method did lend itself in an obvious way to computerization—after all, generative linguistics emulates mathematics as closely as possible—the traditional method could be thought of more as an art in itself. Experts in the field often disagree about particular scansions, and their opposing arguments about a passage involve aspects of the language far beyond the strictly lexical. In making a traditional scansion, you can't entirely ignore the meaning of the passage. This makes it more plausible to argue that the scansion, in turn, will tell you something about the meaning. That makes scansion a tool of literary criticism of an interesting kind. And it also focuses attention, again, on the boundaries of what is computable.

Schoolchildren used to learn how to scan verse. Today, graduate students in English often have to be taught it. The program I wrote will scan iambic pentameter about as well as a good student after a semester's work.

When I set out to teach the computer to scan, naturally I drew on my experience of teaching people to do it. I had worked out a more or less foolproof order of steps to follow in scanning a line of iambic pentameter. Whether I myself follow these steps in order when I scan poems remains an open question. But here's how a student or a program can set out to do it:

1. Look up in the dictionary all the words with more than one syllable, to find out where the main stress in each one falls, and mark it. (/). For the computer, this means asking the user about syllables and stress position in each unknown word and storing the answers in an internal dictionary.

2. Place stresses (/) on the obviously important one-syllable words—generally, all nouns, verbs, adjectives, adverbs, and interjections, but not conjunctions or pronouns or prepositions. For this purpose, the computer asks the user about the unknown word's part of speech and again stores this in its dictionary.

3. Mark all the rest of the syllables as unstressed, or "slack" (x). To do this, you again have to know how many syllables the word has. This is difficult to deduce in English (spelling is quirky and linguistic history is tangled: a word like *aged* may be one syllable or two depending on whether it describes a man or a cheese), but the information is now stored in the computer's dictionary.

4. Divide this string of preliminary marks into feet (|). This is the hard part, where logical complexities and special knowledge come in. Both the student and the computer expend most of their energy and make most of their mistakes in this stage.

5. Write out the finished scansion above the line itself. This is a

trivial problem for the student. But the computer, to line the marks up with the words, must store not only the number of syllables but the positions of the boundaries between them, must deal with blank spaces, punctuation between words, and proportionally spaced fonts. Here's where the human, always a whiz at visual pattern recognition, beats the pants off the computer.

The difficulties of step 4 are the especially interesting ones. To see why, let's go back to that important distinction between *meter* (which is an abstract pattern

de-DUM de-DUM de-DUM de-DUM de-DUM

that lies unchanging behind all the individual lines) and *rhythm*, which varies from any particular line to any other. In "The curfew tolls the knell of parting day" (Thomas Gray), the similar sounds and meanings of "tolls" and "knell" clinch the line around a strong center. In "The trim of pride, the impudence of wealth" (Alexander Pope), sound and grammar group the first and third nouns and the second and fourth. This and a dozen other details distinguish the rhythms of the two lines, though they're identical in meter.

(We're about to stray into some technicalities involving lovely but inscrutable words like *anapest*. If these don't ring a bell, the reader can take them as magic spells and not worry. The general line of argument, which I hope will be clear, is what's important.)

The influence of the speech-based rhythm on the abstract pattern of meter shows up in "metrical substitutions." Trochees (/ x), anapests (x x /), spondees (/ /), or other combinations get substituted for the predominant iambs (x /). Here's a line by W. B. Yeats (from "No Second Troy") with three substitutions:

x / | x / | x x / | / / | x x /

Have taught to ignorant men most violent ways

The syncopated rhythm of the words pushes against the regular beat of the metrical pattern, forcing an accommodation that shows up in the third, fourth, and fifth feet of the scansion. When we listen to the line in its context in the poem, we hear both rhythm and meter at once, jostling against each other in a lively way. Among other things, the line's metrical handling tells us to equate "ignorance" with "violence."

Conversely, the metrical pattern influences the rhythm the line has when spoken. This shows up in "promoted stresses"—syllables not much emphasized in speech but stressed by the meter. In scansion these are sometimes marked "(/)"; but to facilitate the final step (5) in the sequence (printing the result), I used a one-character mark: "%". Here's a line of Wordsworth's with two promoted stresses (as well as one substitution):

$$x \quad / \mid / \quad / \mid x \quad \% \mid x \quad / \mid x \quad \%$$
A sight so touching in its majesty

"In" and the last syllable of "majesty" aren't strongly stressed, but the meter encourages us to hear them as more strongly stressed than the syllables that flank them.

Because of the two kinds of possible variation, a line can be *irregular* without being *unmetrical*. In English metrical verse, this kind of licensed rule-bending is a main source of rhythmic liveliness. Sometimes, as in Yeats's line about ignorant violence, the variations can very directly create meaning.

These two kinds of variations—substitutions and promotions—create many ambiguities about where to place the divisions between feet in an irregular line. Both the number of syllables and the number and position of stresses can vary. Most of these ambiguities can be resolved by means of a set of rules—not a brief set but certainly not infinite in number or in subtlety.

These rules, deduced from the practice of poets throughout history and sometimes no more than statistical generalizations, are what I was interested in making explicit by building them into the logic of a program. The procedure called FootDiv was by far the longest in the program. I'll give just one concrete example of the kind of problem that took a while to iron out.

The program checks first to see if a line is "headless"—that is, if it begins with a single stressed syllable. This isn't uncommon. If the

line is only nine syllables long and if the first three syllables are / x /,
then it's a good bet, and the program proceeds on that assumption:

/ | x / | x / | x / | / /

Autumn gives us hours to think things through.

But suppose the line begins with /x/ but is ten syllables long, like
a normal iambic pentameter? There are two main possibilities. It
might go like this:

/ x / x / x / x x /

Winter shakes the restless fire in the grate

Or it might go:

/ x / / x / x / x /

Give me three reasons why the summer ends

or any of several other variations. The first one should be treated as
headless:

/ | x / | x / | x / | x x /

Winter shakes the restless fire in the grate

(Why not "/ x | / x | / x | / x | x /"? Because even two trochaic
substitutions in a row are quite unusual, and four would make the
line hopelessly unstable. The "headless" reading is much more natu-
ral, meaning that it's a much simpler match between the rhythm and
the metrical pattern.) But the second line —

/ x | / / | x / | x / | x /

Give me three reasons why the summer ends

—won't work if you try to make it headless. (One of the remaining
feet will have to be either x / / or / x /, neither of which is a "legal"
substitution. Legal? Well, rarely. The first is called a bacchius and is
occasionally found as a substitution for the anapest (x x /) in verse
whose normal base-foot is the anapest. The second is called a cretic or
amphimacer and does show up occasionally in some irregular iambic
verse. The Byzantine complexity of traditional metrical theory can
itself be an idle pleasure. Even more, in some moods one can love the
wonderful sound of all the *names*.)

How can the program tell these two instances apart without de-
generating into an endless list of special cases? The best answer turns
out to be a two-stage approach. In the initial test for headless lines,

reject all of these ten-syllable cases; treat them as normal. The second example ("Give me three reasons") can be scanned successfully that way. But at the end of the foot-division process, the first line ("Winter shakes") will be caught by a new final test: Any line that begins with more than one trochee in a row gets turned into a headless line instead. So / x | / x | / x | / x | x / will be corrected to / | x / | x / | x / | xx/.

All these shenanigans required a program about eight hundred lines long—not all that large. (The routine that handled the internal dictionary took up almost as much of it as the foot-division calculations.) It performed surprisingly well. Here's Shakespeare's Sonnet 116:

/ | x / | x x / | x x | / /
Let me not to the marriage of true minds
x / | x / | x % | / x | / /
Admit impediments; love is not love
x / | x % | x%|x / | x /
Which alters when it alteration finds,
x / | x % | x / | x % | x /
Or bends with the remover to remove.
/ / | x %|x /|x / | x /
O no, it is an ever fixed mark
x / | x / | x % | x / | x / x
That looks on tempests and is never shaken;
x% | x / | x / | x / | x x /
It is the star to every wandering bark,
x / | x / | x / | x / | x / x
Whose worth's unknown, although his height be taken.
/ / | / / | x /|x / | x /
Love's not Time's fool, though rosy lips and cheeks
x / | x / | x / | x / | x /
Within his bending sickle's compass come,
/ / | x / | x x | / / | x /
Love alters not with his brief hours and weeks,

x   / | x / | /x |x x / | x /

But bears it out even to the edge of doom.

x % | x / | x %|x / | x /

If this be error and upon me proved,

x /|x   / | x /| / /|x /

I never writ, nor no man ever loved.

This is not an easy poem to scan, as my students have often complained. And there's nothing in the computer's scansion that I'd mark *wrong* in a student paper, though there are lines that I would scan differently. (I read the fourth line as "Or *bends with* the remover to remove.")

Even a highly irregular poem like Yeats's "The Second Coming" falls pretty well within the program's scope. it deals calmly with lines like these:

/   x | x / | x % |x / |x x /

Turning and turning in the widening gyre . . .

and

x   / | x % | x x / | x % | x /

The ceremony of innocence is drowned . . .

and even

x   /| x   / | x   /|x x / | /   /

The Second Coming! Hardly are those words out

x x | / / |x / |x /|x x / x

When a vast image out of Spiritus Mundi

/ x |x / | /   x |x / | x x / x

Troubles my sight: somewhere in sands of the desert . . .

But I would quarrel with the program's handling of this line from Yeats's "No Second Troy":

x   x | / / | x%|x x   / | x %

That is not natural in an age like this . . .

And in "The Second Coming," the program prints an "I GIVE UP" message at the end of the line, "A shape with lion body and the head of a man."

These two different failures have a common cause. The line from

"No Second Troy" would be more accurate if the promoted stress fell on the monosyllabic "in," rather than on the end of "natural." The line from "The Second Coming" can't be scanned at all unless the end of "body" and the "and" are *elided*—treated as a single unstressed syllable—which depends on the knowledge that "body" ends with a vowel and "and" begins with one and that elision has been conventionally acceptable in various periods of literary history.

Why can't the program learn these details? Or rather, why would it have to be radically rebuilt to learn them? Adding a new idea like elided syllables isn't that hard for a human student.

One answer is that most computers can only do one thing at a time, and this forces the programmer to break a process down into discrete steps. (To a smaller degree, teaching encourages the same thing. That's how I came up with my list of five steps toward scansion.) When you add the steps before and after the actual scansion that the computer needs to have made explicit, the full procedure includes

1. reducing the words to a preliminary series of stress and slack marks with the help of the dictionary.
2. deducing from the line of marks an array of five foot-codes,
3. retranslating the foot-codes into expanded and corrected scansion marks, and
4. correlating the final scansion marks with the words again.

But this procedure means that lexical information, information about the words *as words*, is invisible in the middle stages. And the problems in those two lines involve exactly that relation between the scansion marks and the words themselves.

The computer could theoretically be made to switch gears at this point—to go back to a lexical view of the line and use that to correct the narrow logic of scansion marks. It would be a big project. But more important, I don't know how to tell the computer *when* to do this. When is lexical information relevant (aside from these two particular cases I happened to run across)? I don't know how I know that, so I don't know how to tell the computer to decide. There are "expert system" AI programs that handle this kind of problem, a what's-relevant problem. (Medical diagnostics is an area where this approach gets applied.) These are, to say the least, bigger programs than I'd like to undertake.

Even within the foot-division logic, the order of different tests and operations makes a tricky difference. Go back to that problem of the "headless" line I mentioned earlier. The first line of Shakespeare's sonnet, "Let me not to the marriage of true minds," presents metrical problems even for human scholars. But pity the computer that had to follow these steps, as in an earlier version of my program:

1. Detect / x / at the opening and mark off a defective foot plus an iamb, no matter what the line's length.
2. Now, seeking three feet among seven remaining syllables,

x x / x x / /
("to the marriage of true minds")

take the one extra syllable as a clue to look for an anapest (x x /).
3. Pick the pattern / x x / as the best candidate for the position of the anapest: / | x x /. (This rule usually works quite well.)
4. Identify the preceding foot as another anapest—the only possibility.
5. Give up in despair on the last foot:

/ | x / | x x / | x x / | ?
Let me not to the marriage of true minds

Failures of this kind led me to revise the sequence this way:

1. Detect / x / at the beginning, but note that the line is not a syllable short (like the simplest kind of headless line).
2. Finding no other major exceptions, divide the line into two-syllable units as usual: / x | / x | x / | x x | / /
3. Reviewing the completed scansion, notice the highly unusual double trochees at the beginning. Replace them and the succeeding iamb with a defective foot, an iamb, and an anapest: / | x / | x x / | x x | / /

Experiment shows that this system discriminates more accurately between different cases. The rules it embodies turn out to be more general, applicable to more lines. Even so, some literary critics (Helen Vendler, notably) might argue convincingly that the more unusual scansion, the double-trochee opening, is the right one for this unusual, abrupt opening line. The computer can't join in or settle debates of that kind—though by forcing us to specify the rules explicitly, it might have a few points to contribute.

Even when it comes to problems of the other kind, flaws in the very structure of the program's algorithm (or computational procedure), I'm not saying that solutions are impossible, that we've found the point where scansion becomes noncomputable. Instead, the solutions would require a different approach to programming and another order of programming effort. That in turn tells us something about the kind of knowledge we're bringing to bear when we scan a line of verse.

The most interesting point about this program may be the way it partially refutes my original assumption. I began by saying that traditional scansion requires an awareness of the meaning of the words. As we've seen, I can occasionally trace a disagreement between my own scansion and the computer's scansion to its failure to *read* the line in any real sense. Where its logic produces this,

x / | / x | /x | x % | x /

A gaze blank and pitiless as the sun,

I might note instead how sound and meaning isolate the adjective "blank," and scan

x / | / | x / | xx % | x /

A gaze blank and pitiless as the sun.

Similarly, in Shakespeare's sonnet, it's only a feeling for what the line means that would make us read "That bends with the remover to remove," rather than the more regular rhythm scored by the computer's scansion. Yet in the large majority of cases, the mechanical application of foot-division rules succeeds as well as the subtlest human sensitivity to rhythmic nuance. As a system, scansion usually just isn't complicated enough to need a human being.

Once I had finished the Scansion Machine to this level of performance, I was at a loss as to what to do with it. This was the purest of pure research. What use did it have? It wasn't likely to become a software bestseller. I could distribute it as a public-domain program, but to whom? Who needed an automated iambic pentameter scanner?

Nobody. If the program had a purpose, it was to show that it could do what it did: that traditional scansion could, within certain interesting limits, be automated. The logical next step wasn't to distribute the program but to present it in an article in some technical journal—if I could find the right sort of journal—which I never got around to doing.

But the programming work I had put into my Scansion Machine could go to another purpose as well. It might be linked to my second big programming project. Though it was too big and never finished, it's a relevant one to describe.

The second project was a text editor—"word processor" would be too grand a term—meant especially for poets. It had several features that writers of verse would prize, though nobody else had ever missed them in the many excellent word processing programs available commercially. Since verse is by definition language in lines, my program's special ways of manipulating text had to do with the kinds of things poets do with lines.

Part of the legacy of Modernism, especially the American version of Modernism we owe to William Carlos Williams, is an understanding of how much lineation has to do with what a poem means. To a reader who is listening, there's a big difference between

> when I turn
> my eyes away

and

> when I turn my eyes
> away

Writers of "free verse" often revise poems in important ways without changing a word, just by changing the way the lines are broken and distributed on the page. The lineation helps the poet control how the reader hears the poem, and carefully controlled rhythm governs the very meaning of the words that make it up.

So poets spend a lot of time manipulating lines. Most word processing programs aren't set up for this. They're meant for prose, and they work best on prose units—words, sentences, paragraphs. To do something like

                  dropping part of a line down vertically takes quite a
few keystrokes. To break a line
        In the middle (and perhaps
        Capitalize it), which is a single
                      logical operation
        In the mind of the poet, requires

several separate steps. Rejoining two lines is even more tedious. When one mental operation has to be broken into a series of stages, the writer's concentration gets dissipated. So my text editor made these line manipulations easier.

But it went beyond that by incorporating the main feature of the earlier Sinclair ZX81 program: randomness. This time the point wasn't to generate random poems. The point was for the writing machine—a sort of glorified typewriter—to offer the poet as much help as it could in its humble mechanical way. One kind of help that poets do sometimes need is a kind of jolt, something to stir the mind's waters out of lassitude and placidity.

Traditionally, the stringent requirements of meter and rhyme have played this part. Having to match a rhyme often makes the poet shift the poem's stream in an unintended, serendipitous direction. Some poets use other texts as springboards, either incorporating them as quotations or taking off from them in ways that the reader never sees.

My new version of this technique was called the Hoard. You could type in a lot of fragments (phrases, single words, half-lines) and store them in a sort of treasury. Then, when you were writing a poem, if you got stuck and wanted an external, unpredictable impulse, one keystroke would call up a fragment from the hoard at random and insert it into your poem. Of course, you might immediately delete it (there was a one-key command for that, too). But in the meantime it might have given you another, more suitable impulse.

I called the whole program, including the Hoard and the text editor, AleaPoem. "Alea" is the Latin word for "dice"; aleatory composers leave some elements of their music or its performance up to chance processes like rolling dice.

My next thought was to incorporate the Scansion Machine into AleaPoem. Most word processors now include spelling checkers. While you're typing, you can press a key to ask whether you've spelled a word correctly or to check the spelling throughout the document. AleaPoem would have a "meter checker" that worked the same way. Writing or revising a metrical line, you could ask for a scansion of it.

Even this planned version of the editor wouldn't write poems. It would automate as much of the poetry-writing process as could be automated. The question I was exploring was, how much of the process might that be? Once I understood that the Scansion Machine could be part of AleaPoem, I knew an answer to that question. I stopped there without doing it—still dreaming.

After all, why go on? The research part was done. As for implementation, I had to ask: If I were successful, what difference would it make? No one who read a poem written with the help of AleaPoem would be able to tell what had gone into it. A poem's meaning is all on its surface, in the sense that if no reader can see it, it doesn't effectively exist. My editor might possibly make some aspects of writing easier, but that in itself is no interesting virtue. I'm a poet, not a software entrepreneur. (And no entrepreneur would bet his shirt on a word processor for poets.) I was growing interested in making a computer make a difference in a poem. To do that I needed a new approach.

TRAVESTY

In November 1984, Hugh Kenner, the great Modernist literary critic, and his colleague at Johns Hopkins, the computer scientist Joseph O'Rourke, published an article in *Byte* magazine called "A Travesty Generator for Micros."

Neither literary scholars nor computer science professors publish often in microcomputer magazines. Kenner and O'Rourke were both playing hookey, from different schools. (It's worth noting, though, that Kenner had already written on Buckminster Fuller's mathematics and on the relevance of group theory to poetry.) Naturally enough, the article's claims on its readers' interest are divided.

On the one hand, the authors are demonstrating the implementation of algorithms (that is, computational procedures) for pattern matching that were first suggested by Brian P. Hayes in the "Computer Recreations" column of *Scientific American* a year earlier. Most of the *Byte* article is devoted to details of the algorithm and its implementation, with discussion of ways to improve efficiency. The article inspired an unusual number of letters to *Byte*'s editor, and most of them offered programming improvements and alternatives.

On the other hand, the purpose of the program itself is to generate "travesty" texts from other texts so as to examine the relation between the original and its transformation and deduce various things about the language of the original. In short, Travesty is a computer stylistics program.

Here's what the program does. A text, such as a passage from a novel, is among other things a set of characters. It consists of so many *e*'s, so many f's, and so on. It's also a set of character pairs (so many *ex*'s, so many *ch*'s, etc.) and of triplets (*the*'s, *wkw*'s, etc.), and so on.

For any same-size group of characters—call the size n—it's possible to make a frequency table for a particular text. From that table, another text can be constructed that shares statistical properties, but only those properties, with the first one. That's what Travesty does. It produces an output text that duplicates the frequencies of n-character groups in the input text. To put the same thing the other way, it thoroughly scrambles its input text but only down to level n.

At n = 1 all you get is a mishmash of letters that more or less obeys the usual frequency distribution of English. (E is the most frequent letter, t is next, and so on). If you set n equal to 2, the result is slightly more organized gibberish:

> Dengethe pr: o ls h thee. wicach Ye thur. obbug lesila thi-catetonoisthate Thrit O athe are. t is: winsict kerprurise, y m? th o mor sty hetseatheancathensous.

The longest pattern-matching string allowed by the original Travesty is nine characters. At n = 9, the output text largely duplicates the input text—except for some odd leaps. Here's the beginning of the tenth chapter of the book of Ecclesiastes:

> Dead flies cause the ointment of the apothecary to send forth a stinking savour: so doth a little folly him that is in reputation for wisdom and honour. A wise man's heart is at his right hand; but a fool's heart at his left. . . .

And here's an n = 9 travesty (using the whole chapter as an input text):

> Dead flies cause the ointment of the ruler: folly is set in great dignity, and the end of his mouth is foolishness: and the end of his talk is mischievous madness. A fool also is full of words: a man cannot tell what shall bite him. Whoso removeth stones shall be endangered thereby. If the iron be blunt, and he do not whet the edge, then must he put to more strength: but wisdom is profitable to direct.

The last sentence in this passage remains perfectly intact. If it sounds strange—well, that's one of the program's effects on our reading. On the other hand, the "ointment of the ruler," though it sounds plausible, is a figment. The program has compounded it from "ointment of the apothecary" and "spirit of the ruler" by way of the repeated nine-character run (including blanks), t of the .

Formally, as Kenner and O'Rourke point out, "The connection of the output to the source can be stated exactly: for an order-n scan, every n-character sequence in the output occurs somewhere in the input, and at about the same frequency."

The authors use Travesty to make a number of paradoxical points about language. (We may hear Kenner's voice as the dominant one in this section of the article.) The frequency distributions characteristic of English determine, without intervention from a writer's conscious thought, a startlingly large proportion of what the writer writes. "In fact, the language makes three-quarters of your writing decisions for you."

It may not be surprising, then, that even when n equals only 3, the emerging output is, though nonsense, clearly English nonsense (again the input is Ecclesiastes):

> Deare thy ings. The thy hedge, afte se the whatter: for so mou, alk iroppen due inch an te in to misdo caught; mants oness! The lisdom the not of an ton, and theast for diggerpenning is shalking! By tall the retheat shat his und, woolips sithe eve len thall bableft. A wisdot sloth, and forength him then rings. For of to ing is man's whildigninch him. Deader: He offen rulefter.

"Misdo" is a real word (hence, "misdeed"). So is "ings," a northern English term for "meadow." Just as Lewis Carroll reinvented "gyre" and "slithy," Travesty has reinvented "ings" and "misdo." Neither of these words, nor the equally valid "sithe," "mants," or "shat," appears in Ecclesiastes. But the English dictionary says they could. And the statistical habits of English designate "woolips" and "diggerpenning" as possible words too, which speakers of English happened never to invent.

Naturally, the grip of statistics grows stronger and stronger as n increases. Of all the possible four-letter groups (zxiq, fmup, qtno), only a tiny minority are available to the writer of English.

And yet free choice remains. Indeed, free choice is all a writer is aware of while writing. But there's more choice than awareness encompasses. Finally, "The *significant* [my emphasis] statistics derive from the personal habits of James, or Joyce, or Jack London, or J. D. Salinger. Each of these writers, amazingly, had his own way with trigrams, tetragrams, pentagrams, matters to which he surely gave no thought." What interests Kenner and O'Rourke about their program is the emergence of these stylistic signatures: "the unexpected fact that essentially random nonsense can preserve many 'personal' characteristics of a source text."

Before inviting us into this sophisticated examination of stylistics, however, Travesty offers more childish pleasures. One of them is implicit in the program's name: It's the wickedness of exploding revered literary scripture into babble. We can reduce Dr. Johnson to inarticulate imbecility, make Shakespeare talk very thickly through his hat, or exhibit Francis Bacon laying waste his own edifice of logic amid the pratfalls of $n = 9$.

Yet the other side of the same coin is a kind of awe. Here is language creating itself out of nothing, out of mere statistical noise. As we raise n, we can watch sense evolve and meaning stagger up onto its own miraculous feet. We can share the sense of wonder that James Joyce aimed at in the "Oxen of the Sun" chapter of *Ulysses*, where the history of the language from grunts to Parliamentary orations unfolds like a morality play before our ears.

Yet it's not clear where this meaning is coming from. Nothing is created out of nothing; and the principles of nonsense discussed in chapter 2 insist that we keep the perceiving reader in his or her place, responsible along with the text and the author for making sense. The reconsideration of these issues belongs to a later stage of my history, and I'll come back to it in the next chapters.

There are two ways to play with this program. If you keep feeding it texts and adjusting n, you can extend the stylistic discoveries of Kenner and O'Rourke—and liven up a late-night party. Or you can take the hint of the printed source code and start tinkering with the program's innards, extending and modifying. As you learn more intimately how the program works (often by making changes that unexpectedly break it), you're bound to start thinking in new detail about what it does.

Messing around with Travesty, I began to see the progressive rousing of sense out of a mindless sea of letters as resembling the evolution of human beings. It certainly wasn't Darwin's version of evolution. Instead, the body—the mechanical corpuscles and ligaments of language—was evolving into mind. Though Darwinian theory has been saddled with this kind of progressivism, it's a misconception. Biological evolution doesn't *go toward anything*, as Stephen Jay Gould often points out. The story I was telling myself was a myth. Any discursive theory behind it would sound like a lot of Cartesian silliness that I didn't believe in for a moment. This didn't stop me from being excited by the drama I was seeing (or making up). The need for *belief* in a myth has never slowed poets down very much; it's what the myth says about things outside itself that matters.

Just at that time I had written a short poem about a famous chess game. Even after I was sure it was finished, the poem didn't seem adequate. For me, that's become a sure sign that the poem at hand is just one section of a larger work. This is a corollary of the Modernist principle of juxtaposition that we've already glimpsed. Most extended modern poems are built in pieces, which the poet composes into a whole without covering up the seams between adjacent parts. I began to add new sections, in different verse forms. They had different starting points, scattered throughout all the reading I was doing at the time; but they converged, as things written at the same time tend to do, under pressure from the same unresolved concerns. As the poem grew, it didn't settle on a clear central theme, but it revealed a constant set of interweaving obsessions: chess, computers, war, the mathematician Alan Turing. None of this process was very unusual for me, and I can't recall exactly when I decided that some Travesty text should be included. But I know I'd been thinking about the Turing Game.

Alan Turing himself called it "the imitation game." The paper that describes it, "Can a Machine Think?" (published in 1950 in the British journal Mind), is one of the important documents of this century, touching on mysteries that intrigue us deeply. Yet some of its details haven't been widely noticed.

The physical setup for the game is simple. Two players, A and B, and a person Turing calls the "interrogator" sit in three separate rooms, communicating by teletype or other impersonal means. The interrogator asks questions and tries to identify A and B. In answering the interrogator's questions, player A tries to imitate player B. Or rather, player A tries to convince the interrogator that he or she or it belongs to the same *category* to which player B insists (truthfully) that she or he or it belongs.

The famous main point of Turing's essay begins when he makes player A (the imitator) a computer, and player B (the one who is imitated) a human being. He uses this situation to formulate the previously vague question "Can a machine think?" Can the computer convince the human interrogator that it too is a human being?

First, though, to explain the game, Turing proposes a different version: Player A is a man who tries to pretend he's a woman; player B is a woman and says so. As Turing's biographer, Andrew Hodges, points out, this was relevant to his own experience of sexual ambiguity in homophobic midcentury England.

Hodges calls this first version of the game

> a red herring, and one of the few passages of the paper that was not expressed with perfect lucidity. The whole point of this game was that a successful imitation of a woman's responses by a man would *not* prove anything. Gender depended on facts which were *not* reducible to sequences of symbols. In contrast, he wished to argue that such an imitation principle did apply to "thinking" or "intelligence."

Hodges's fundamental critique of the essay as a whole is that Turing's isolation of human *intelligence* from the body and senses partly belies the nature of *human* intelligence. In this I believe Hodges is right. But

I'm less convinced by his analysis of the "sexual guessing game." I think he misses the point. Using "gender" in too vague a sense, he assumes that the theorem to be proved or ridiculed is that *men are the same as women*. What I think Turing meant was instead that *sociolinguistic behavior—that is, talk—won't reliably distinguish between a man and a woman*.

This is contrary to what many people assume, consciously or unconsciously. Surely *he* couldn't convince us when it came to clothes. Surely (if the game were reversed—notice that Turing doesn't present it symmetrically), *she'd* give herself away on football. The shrewd interrogator won't just ask how the players feel about the Equal Rights Amendment—ask player A how often "she" drives when "her" husband is in the car.

Turing cuts deeply into our sense of what we know about each other. We've come to understand that much of human reality is linguistic. The names we give things control how we see them. We live in words as fish live in water. But how real is this verbal reality? The game asks: If we can't see or touch or hear a person, how certain can we be about the categories we assign the person to? If our talk lets us define ourselves, it also lets us masquerade. This is one of the fascinations people are discovering on the Internet. They hang out with others from twenty-four time zones, whom they will never see, whose voices they will never hear—people who exist for them only as typed words. The opportunities for confusion and outright fraud are balanced by a certain liberation; racism has a hard time with e-mail.

We often treat socially important categories like gender as absolute. Against this, Turing poses his question in terms of *probability*: "Will the interrogator decide wrongly as often when the game is played like this [between human and machine] as he [sic] does when the game is played between a man and a woman?" And his ultimate prediction is couched in similar terms: Within fifty years (from 1950) a computer with a billion bits of memory—not so very large by today's standards, about 120 megabytes—will be able to win the game in 70 percent of five-minute trials. There's an implication that this is the rate of success he'd expect in the gender game, too. (Has anyone actually tried the gender game?)

Other categories besides gender come to mind: race, class, and so on. As soon as "knowing" is put in terms of "imitation," a fundamental shakiness shows up everywhere in our humanly constituted reality. As I thought about Turing's paper, these questions began to infiltrate my poem in various ways.

Turing notes that if the second version of the game is reversed, it puts the human being at a serious disadvantage. It's far easier for the computer to mimic human slowness and errors in arithmetic (as in an imaginary sample dialogue he gives) than for a human to emulate a computer's speedy accuracy. Yet the history of our uneasy relations with machines—at least since the industrial revolution and Frankenstein and the first saboteurs, who threw their wooden sandals (*sabots*) into machines that were replacing their jobs—is full of odd instances of people imitating machines. An interesting example is "the Turk" (along with its own imitators, like Ajeeb or Coney Island). This was a nineteenth-century "chess-playing machine"—it once chastised Catherine the Great for cheating—in the likeness of a man, which in fact concealed a legless war veteran: an imitation within an imitation.

At a certain point, when I felt I was done with the little poems that would be sections of the big poem, I conglomerated all of them into one computer file and used that text as input for a series of eight runs of Travesty, with $n = 2$, $n = 3$, and so on through $n = 9$. I had altered the program so that (instead of producing an amount of output determined arbitrarily by the user) it would keep going until a period or question mark coincided with the end of a line. I ended up with eight sections that looked vaguely like paragraphs.

I've oversimplified the process in several ways. In the first place, I began trying all this before I was really done with "my" parts of the poem. Whenever I altered one of those, I had to alter the big input file made up of them all, and of course that would alter all the output sections when I reran the program.

It's worth stopping to ask why I felt I had to do that. The output was nonsense anyway; why not just leave it alone? Who'd notice the difference? One reason was that any discrepancies might show up visibly in the output, though that wasn't very likely. No one was going to do the backtracking—theoretically possible but extremely laborious—that would be necessary to show that an output section was or wasn't properly derived from the combined input.

A better reason was simply that it was my rule. It was a little like adhering to a pattern of rhyme and meter. Or maybe, since infractions were unlikely to be detected, it was more like the rules of solitaire. Artists, like artisans, try to get things right, even when it means carving the backs of the gargoyles. Ultimately, I suppose I was so scrupulous about my procedure precisely because I was departing so far from anything my background had prepared me to think of as "writing poetry." I was defending myself, if only to myself, against charges of self-indulgence and laziness. But if you examine this argument closely, you can see that the rules had changed. I was being faithful to something rather new.

A second minor problem that I've skipped over was deciding exactly what would and wouldn't be included in the input text. Arbitrarily, I simplified some punctuation and ignored lineation. All this was to increase the smoothness, the fluidity, and ultimately the plausibility of the output. For instance, omitting all parentheses meant that I wouldn't end up with unmatched right or left parentheses. These were ploys to boost the appearance of sense, the lure of meaningfulness.

By now I knew the title of the poem: "Monologues of Soul and Body." There have been dialogues between the soul and body throughout English literature; Andrew Marvell wrote a wonderful poem of that name. But in this case the body and soul, rather than conversing, talked somehow past each other. The parts I had written myself were the "soul" parts. In the computer output I saw the body constructing itself out of the material of soul, working step by step back toward articulation and coherence. It's a very Idealist poem, and at the same time very Cartesian, and perhaps monstrous.

So as to give my reader at least a hint about what was going on, I decided to open the poem with two epigraphs, one for each group. The "Epigraph of the Body" was Kenner and O'Rourke's formal statement of the relation between Travesty's input and output. The "Possible Epigraphs of the Soul"—plural because the soul was irreducibly in dialogue with itself—quoted the tall-tale teller Maeterlinck in praise of truth. The soul's domain is irony; the body's is reductive fact.

At this point I was faced with a major decision about structure. I decided wrong the first time. I put all eight Travesty paragraphs, in order, together at the end. The result was unreadable—offensively unreadable. My very first reader saved me by pointing this out with considerable force.

The alternative was simply to go one step further in my role as poetic composer: I scattered the eight "Body" sections among the "Soul" sections at what my ear told me were the right places. The vaguely evolutionary idea I had begun with dictated that the eight "Body" sections, though scattered, should remain in order.

This brings me to the final and most interesting problem that I left out in my simplified description of the poem. I've said that I ran my conglomerated input "Soul" file through Travesty eight times. But in fact I was often disappointed with the program's results. If I ran it twice (with n the same both times), I could usually choose one of the results as superior to the other.

Superior how? Sometimes an intriguing combination would crop up (from Ecclesiastes: "Dead for yielding!" "A wise madness!"). Sometimes the program would invent a beautiful word ("avathefomitor," "runkin," "andaneld"). Sometimes a phrase belonging to a later "Soul" section would emerge, provocatively foreshadowed, in an earlier "Body" section. But most often, I chose on the basis that ultimately, and not trivially, governs most poetic decisions: I kept the results that *sounded* best. The fragments came together in pleasing tunes, or attractive rhythms, or evocative echoes of half-apprehended thoughts.

The question was, how many choices should I make? If I could choose the better of two, why not the best of twenty? Of two hundred? The way the program generated random numbers happened to put a limit on the number of candidates (65,536 for each value of n); but multiplied by the eight values of n, it was still a number whose human name is Too Many. In the end, I read nonsense all day for several long days; and when I couldn't read any more, I stuck with the best I'd found.

AUTOPOET

Far beyond the simple RanLines program on the Sinclair ZX81, "Monologues of Soul and Body" raised questions about authorship. Of course I was the author: I wrote most of the sections, gave them their titles, rewrote the published program, laboriously chose eight from a morass of computer outputs, and composed the whole thing as a poem, giving it its title and epigraphs.

But the "Soul" sections are full of quotations; and selecting from among the scrupulously unedited productions of a computer program hardly seems like *writing poetry*. Whatever this was, it wasn't exactly the sort of authorship we attribute to Homer or to Charlie Parker. On the other hand, there's a six-hundred-page dissertation demonstrating that Parker's incredibly inventive playing was based on a thesaurus of melodic formulas—as was Homer's singing.

Questions like this are woven into the fabric of twentieth-century art, as I've pointed out by talking about juxtaposition and collage and composition. The source of some material in my poem was fairly novel, but the poem's overall method wasn't unfamiliar. Even the idea of using a source text as the basis for a poetic text had been around for some time. Jackson Mac Low, Rosmarie Waldrop, William Burroughs, and dozens of others have used various methods to produce one text out of another for years, often with uncannily beautiful results.

"Monologues" is partly *about* the problems of its origin. The "Soul" sections dwell on computers acting like people and vice versa. The poem shows thought devolving into mechanism and a machine struggling toward what looks like thought. It worries about the limits of knowledge and how very close to home they sometimes fall. It mixes facts and other sorts of fictions and expresses distrust about the relation between games like chess and realities like wars.

So I had finally employed a computer in the construction of a poem I found genuinely interesting (and have since embraced by publishing it, first in the experimental magazine *Tyuonyi*, and then in my book of poems from Wesleyan University Press, *Glass Enclosure*). What next?

Coleridge called poetry "the best words in the best order." Glimpsed from this particular angle, a poem is nothing but a selection and arrangement of words from the dictionary. This seems like a potentially mechanizable process. The poet's task can be seen as a problem of scale: there are so very many possible combinations of words to choose among. This gives the poet an enormous practical problem. But aside from that, it's an idea of poetry that makes the poet's chief job *judgment*, not exactly *creation*. This sounds more like an eighteenth-century poet than a nineteenth-century one, more Neoclassical than Romantic. But the twentieth century offers, if nothing else, a choice of ancestors.

What I wanted to do next was to resurrect the Scansion Machine and turn it into a productive engine, rather than a strictly analytic one. If I could find a way to generate candidate lines of verse, the scansion procedure could filter out unmetrical ones. Then I could build a metrical poem out of the victors. It would still be me doing the building. But the computer would be producing the poem's language on its own.

I was seeking a common ground between what the computer (in my amateur programming hands) could realistically do and what I could plausibly define as writing poetry. After "Monologues," how far would I have to go in a different direction to make these ends meet again?

So a program in Pascal began to grow out of the Scansion Machine. At some early stage I named it "Natural Selection." The metaphor I had thought about while writing "Monologues" was still unsatisfied, still looking for expression. Vaguely, I entertained the vision of a horde of lines, a whole population competing for the sustenance of attention—but whose attention? I neither expected nor wanted to write myself out of the picture. Presenting the reader with all the computer's combinations was out of the question. I anticipated making any final selection myself. The question was what it would take, in the way of computer filtering, to reduce an indefinitely large number of possible lines to a flock small enough for me to cull.

The initial problem was to generate the candidates. My first method was to string together words at random until I'd collected the right number of syllables (nine to thirteen, say) for an iambic pentameter.

What words? The commonest words are very common indeed. Without a good proportion of them, no stretch of imitation English has much chance of sounding sensible. So I began by building a dictionary of the few thousand most common words. I used the word-frequency list compiled by Kuçera and Searle from their sample of a million printed English words.

My dictionary added three pieces of information to this list: the number of syllables in the word, the stressed syllable if there was more than one, and the part of speech. These are the same details that the Scansion Machine elicited from the user for each word it came across in the poem to be scanned. This kind of information isn't usually included in the computerized dictionaries used to check spelling; I had to build my own.

The output tended to run like this:

> investigation of the guy the stay
> wrote great the seeing the blue particular
> wonderful services repeated remember
> the summer more vision with the wet past
> division in the none traditional
> universe appeared generally day
> settled early the complex feel the dropped
> the early reality is nuclear

and so on. Disappointing, to say the least. Obviously, mere random selection wasn't enough.

In fact I had already introduced heavy statistical weighting into the program's random choices. Words from the first group of five hundred were chosen far more often than any of the rest. Within the first group the choice was still further guided by an algebraic function with a very steep curve (one over x squared, plus one) that roughly approximates the curve of frequencies in actual English. I also added a group of five hundred "specials," words I hand-picked for interest. These were inserted unusually often.

None of it helped. The nonsense factor was working far too well. Even the most willing reader—and I was still pretty willing, even after thrashing around in the output of Travesty—couldn't make much sense of these lines, especially in combination. For the next step I'd have to add syntax.

I have great faith in syntax. Language is sentences, not words, and not simple word frequencies. I've heard (though I've heard other linguists dispute it) that children learn syntax even before they learn vocabulary. Certainly, my son uttered little tunes that contained no recognizable words but sounded like speech. I could almost, but not quite, understand him. He was meaning to speak. Writing and reading poems drives home the conviction that it's not the words alone that create voice and image, power and meaning, but the relations among them. Meter makes one kind of relation among words, but syntax relates them in a far more pervasive and subtle way. Where there's syntax, there ought to be meaning. Or at least, to state my hope more exactly, enough syntax ought to tempt a reader to help make sense.

But the syntactical system of English is complex. Major research efforts by computer science labs and by linguists, together and separately, haven't come up with a complete formulation of the rules of English syntax. Researchers don't even agree about what such a formulation would look like if we had it. Where those angels were treading on each other's toes, I wasn't fool enough to intrude.

Actually, I realized, what I needed wasn't anything like that. Those researchers were all trying to understand English; I merely wanted to write it. The Imitation Game sharpens your eye for shortcuts. In this case, I was playing the much easier half of the game. Unlike almost all computer programs, the one I envisioned would have no input. It would just utter its language like an oracle, leaving the job of meaning making to the reader's instinctively intelligent questioning.

Notice, by the way, that in this game the computer reverses the human tendency. We can gather a pretty good "passive vocabulary" in a language long before we become fluent speakers. But it's a lot easier to make a computer talk than listen.

At first I tried piecemeal fixes. If the last word chosen at random was an article, make the next one a noun. If a pronoun comes up, follow it with a verb. These patches didn't work well. For example, the rules I've just given exclude all article-adjective-noun combinations (like "a rude awakening"). I tried a variation in which I recast all the rules in negative terms. It was better but not good enough. I needed a real grammar.

The available literature on artificial intelligence is beginning to reach a level the determined nonspecialist can understand. How-to books have accumulated particularly around the language called Prolog, which is especially suited to AI projects like handling what are called grammar networks. My next step should be to vary and extend some of the example programs given in these books. (This is what I'd done with Travesty, altering it toward my purposes. It's how a lot of computer investigations begin. Poets, too, often prime the pump by loosely imitating earlier poems.)

I was learning Prolog at the same time and trying to preserve the work I'd already done. The result of this tinkering was truly a monster, a program written in two pieces in two very different languages that could communicate only with the greatest discomfort. For low computer comedy, here's the headnote to that version: "This version of the Natural Selection program collaborates with (indeed runs as a subtask of) a Prolog program whose function is to create sentence templates. Communication between the programs is by means of a disk file called 'TEMPLATE.' The main parts of the complete system are interrelated [as shown in figure 1.]"

Oddly, the poor thing worked; it would produce one or two lines per minute. Dr. Moreau, too, in the horror story by H. G. Wells, got his beasts to walk on two legs.

I had fallen victim to a kind of purism. Programmers live within an

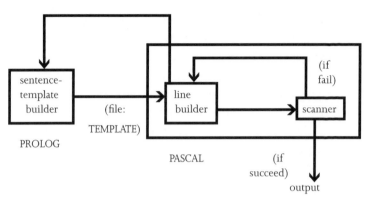

Figure 1

intricate class system of computer languages. Prolog was the Right Language for the template-generating job, so I used Prolog. But my program wasn't big enough to demand that kind of efficiency. I was not doing AI research. Better to fool around in a usable language like Pascal.

So I tore the thing apart and rebuilt it. How it manipulated grammar rules is something I'll describe in more detail in the next chapter because it's the main feature I preserved in the Prose project that finally made something useful out of this mess. But the rest of the program, now called AutoPoet, worked straightforwardly:

1. Create a syntactical skeleton or template—a list of parts of speech in sentence order (e.g., determiner, adjective, noun, verb).

2. Pick words at random from lists of determiners, adjectives, nouns, verbs, and so on, to build a sentence on this template (e.g., "this fatal strop commutes").

3. When the words have accumulated to about the length of a pentameter, test it for metricality.

4. If it passes the test in step 3, print it. If it doesn't, go back to step 2.

The only remaining trick is to preserve the state of the program somewhere around step 2 so that step 4 can return to that point

VIRTUAL MUSE

without losing the grammatical thread of the sentence. That is, we want the sentence to continue even when the line has been successfully completed. This will have the additional advantage of *enjambing* many lines, making them run over in sense. Enjambment gives metrical lines much of their supple liveliness. To accomplish this, there's a lot of information to preserve and, if necessary (if a trial line fails the meter test), to restore: the template, the point reached in the template before the failing candidate line was built, the then-current state of plurality, person, number, and so on. Furthermore, since either a line can end while a sentence is still incomplete or a sentence can end partway through a line, restarting a line can get complicated.

Did it work? No, not very well:

> The garden of steel—place—had figured in
> this. When I am every afternoon,
> how can't the last teacher write? But I
> was art without my play between a result
> and the metabolism, and the night
> of language toward a story between the part
> and any light (the thin subject) remains.
> Unless their jazz among so national
> a center burned to practice, history
> is a machine's afternoon. So sure a plane:
> hotel. The hell of day determines her.
> Because they turn to someone, history
> is so thin a science. The club—so democratic
> a list—is the earth of length. Because the fight
> of clay has met his willow, whom is so straight
> a line determining? While I might compute
> its night, I am the room, and that day plane
> (that garden) had based practice. Will its second
> kill so professional a game? So black a
> jazz stopped to think sound for the range of women,
> and voice—the gas of night through your device—
> was working.

Variations suggested themselves. I even wrote one elaborate version of the program that passed its sentence template through a version of Travesty before filling in the words at random. The result was somewhat interesting—but only if you knew where it had come from.

That was the fundamental problem. The fact that my program worked at all was a little surprising. But it didn't work well enough. I could remain intrigued as the programmer but not as a poet. I had arrived at a barrier where many computer poetry experiments have died of ennui. The Imitation Game is hard to play on humans' home turf, language. All my metrical and syntactical drubbing of the language did only a little to drive the random words toward sense.

Maybe I should have taken this as a victory. As a human poet, I could still do something my computer proved simply incapable of doing. Emerson had said that "it is not meters, but a meter-making argument that makes a poem." I should have listened to him and known better. But it's a pretty cheap victory. If that were the point, I would never have tried the experiments in the first place. If the result is merely a round of congratulations that the human club remains closed to outsiders, all these efforts are pointless.

I was sure I had had a point. I began to think that the fault lay not so much in the computer program but in what I was trying to make it do.

AutoPoet embodied an inappropriate idea of poetry. As long as the goal was the imitation of a human poet—or as long as the poem's reader was encouraged to think that was the goal—I wasn't likely to get any farther. What's wrong with the AutoPoetry I've quoted here (and all the other reams of it the machine would produce until it was turned off) is exactly that it's *imitation poetry*. All our habits of reading are called upon, all the old expectations, and then let down. "Monologues of Soul and Body" had worked because its "body" sections were so *different* from human poetry. It had successfully demanded its own way of reading. To go on from there, once again I needed a new idea.

>>>> / **7** /

PROSE

The next programming project I'll present is in some ways the climax of this book. It's the longest in sheer number of program lines. And while though the idea behind it isn't original, the program does more to *originate* poetry than any of the others.

Yet it represented a kind of retrenchment after the elaborations of AutoPoet. Conceptually, what I did was to remove the iambic pentameter filtering of output text. The remaining program functions coordinated the contents of a dictionary and a grammar, each of them a text file that could be edited separately. The program now produced a sequence of grammatically correct English sentences. Feeling chastened, I called it Prose.

By the time I got to Prose, the dictionary-and-grammar-handling routines had been through at least four major revisions in Natural Section and AutoPoet. I had rewritten them in three different computer languages (Prolog, Pascal, and C). By now they worked smoothly.

Prose offers a "show tree" option. I built this in to help me in debugging the program while I wrote it. But it also exhibits some interesting information in its own right. If this option is turned on, the output looks something like what is shown in figure 2.

Everything between the "=tree=" and "=end=tree=" markers shows the program at work building the syntactical template. Then it builds the actual sentence (about "the order of harm") by randomly selecting words of the right types from the dictionary. To see in more detail how Prose works, let's look at some pieces of this "grammar tree."

The metaphor of a tree is used in linguistics as well as in program-

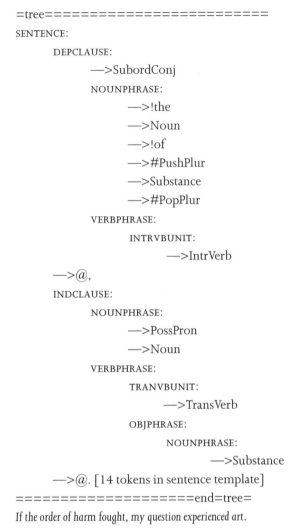

```
=tree=========================
SENTENCE:
    DEPCLAUSE:
        —>SubordConj
        NOUNPHRASE:
            —>!the
            —>Noun
            —>!of
            —>#PushPlur
            —>Substance
            —>#PopPlur
        VERBPHRASE:
            INTRVBUNIT:
                —>IntrVerb
    —>@,
    INDCLAUSE:
        NOUNPHRASE:
            —>PossPron
            —>Noun
        VERBPHRASE:
            TRANVBUNIT:
                —>TransVerb
            OBJPHRASE:
                NOUNPHRASE:
                    —>Substance
    —>@. [14 tokens in sentence template]
=====================end=tree=
```

If the order of harm fought, my question experienced art.

Figure 2

ming. (This is no accident, but what the coincidence means depends on whether you ask a programmer or a linguist.) If you turned this diagram of a sentence on its side and skewed it picturesquely, it could be seen as having a trunk and a lot of branches terminating in leaves (figure 3).

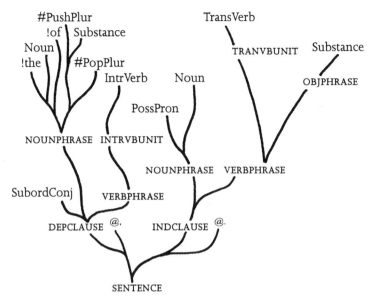

Figure 3

The trunk is the basic unit, Sentence. The process always begins with that. The leaves are the components that finally go into the sentence template itself. In the program's version of the tree diagram, printed earlier, each leaf is indicated by an arrow: —>. So Sentence doesn't become part of the template, but "SubordConj" (for "subordinating conjunction") does, along with "!the" and "@,".

Some of these template units begin with signs that indicate special functions. The "@" indicates punctuation—here, the comma in the middle of the sentence and the period at its end. The "!" indicates a literal, that is, a word that's to be inserted into the sentence as it is, rather than a type of word to be looked up in the dictionary. Literals are especially useful for placing whole phrases in the grammar, like "the A of B," which might be encoded, "!the Noun !of Noun." This is often easier than encoding the proper treatment of phrases (especially idioms) in the program itself.

A "#" indicates a flag—a signal to the sentence-building routines to perform some special task. These flags get complicated in specialized ways, but I'll give a quick explanation of the two that appear in the sample template, "#PushPlur" and "#PopPlur."

Think for a moment how plurality (number) works in sentences. Number gets established somehow—for instance by the subject of the sentence, a noun that is either singular or plural. When we get to the verb, we have to remember the number and make the verb agree with the subject. If we began with "The dog," we have to continue with "dances," not "dance." In between the subject and the verb, though, might come another phrase ("whose teeth are shining"). This phrase too has to be internally consistent in number (not "teeth is"). But no law says it has to be the same in number as the clause it's interrupting. So as we're speaking, inventing the sentence, we *suspend* the state of plurality for a moment, then *restore* it when the digression is over.

In other words, plurality works like the data structure known to programmers as a "stack." "Pushing" and "popping" are the operations that put something onto a stack and take something off it. The usual metaphor is of cafeteria plates in a spring-loaded dispenser. The program suspends plurality by "pushing" the current state (singular or plural) onto the stack. Then a new plurality can be established and govern its phrase without destroying the old information. When the phrase is over, we "pop" the old plurality off the stack to make it active again, ready for the upcoming verb. Sometimes there are several nested levels of plurality in a sentence. ("The dog, whose teeth shine as the moon does, dances.")

The program itself knows only words, not phrase structures. So the grammar (which is kept in a separate text file for easy editing) has to control shifts in the level of plurality. "#PushPlur" and "#Pop-Plur" are the flags that let it do that. Other flags do similar jobs of passing messages from the grammar to the program.

A program really smart about human language would know about things like phrases. It would have a *memory* for suspended items like plurality. Putting this information by hand into the grammar is cheating, as far as AI programming is concerned. But I wasn't concerned about purity in the programming. I just wanted to produce unpredictable but fruitful linguistic material. The fact that I would renounce laziness in the poetry, and not in the programming, just confirmed my sense of proportion and values.

Let's look back at the sentence tree I showed earlier, the odd horizontal one the program prints out. The horizontal indentations in it stand for the layers of a syntactical hierarchy. Each vertically aligned group corresponds to one of the rules in the grammar file. For instance, the Sentence shown earlier is made up of four parts: a dependent clause, a comma, and an independent clause followed by a period. In the grammar, this rule is written:

SENTENCE/ DEPCLAUSE @, INDCLAUSE @.

When the program prints a tree, it arranges these four elements one above the other.

The DepClause, in turn, is made up of a SubordConj, a NounPhrase, and a VerbPhrase. The hierarchy continues until all the constituents of every level are "leaves" that aren't defined by further "branches." The formal way to express this exhaustive nesting of rules depending on other rules is to call the process recursive. Recursion is important in computing; it's also essential to the structure of human languages. We all speak sentences made up of clauses made up of phrases made up of other phrases made up of words. (Only the words come out of our mouths, but the phrases and clauses really exist.) Linguists have shown that we do this by applying grammar rules recursively.

Another sentence might be just an IndClause and a period: "SENTENCE/ INDCLAUSE @." Still another might be an IndClause followed by a semicolon and another sentence. Other sentences are questions, which require different forms from declarations. The grammar contains many rules that define sentences.

Similarly, there are two kinds of VerbPhrase in this sentence: one intransitive (made up of an intransitive verb unit, IntrVbunit—in this case, simply an intransitive verb) and one transitive (made up in this case of a transitive verb unit and an object phrase). In the tree these verb phrases are shown as further indented vertical groups.

When one rule (like the one that defines Sentence) calls for another rule (like one that will define a VerbPhrase), the program chooses *at random* among all the rules of that type in its grammar—all the rules that define the part being called for. This sentence needed two VerbPhrases, and randomly chose different rules for them. If the grammar contains six VerbPhrase rules, each will be chosen about one-sixth of the time. Originally, the odds could be loaded by repeating a favorite rule several times in the grammar. Later I added a "weight" factor to each rule for greater efficiency.

A side note: I've said before that human choices can be arbitrary but not random. And even the "random" numbers in computer programs aren't truly random, like the decay times of elementary particles. They are generated by functions that produce an unpredictable sequence but that, beginning from the same "seed" number, will reproduce the same sequence. The sequence repeats after a certain point—usually, the largest number available in some unit of computer storage, often 65,536. My recent Macintosh-based MacProse uses this fact to advantage. The program usually displays the tree of the most recently generated sentence. When the user clicks the mouse on an earlier sentence, the program reconstructs the tree to display by reseeding the random-number generator with the original value and running its sequence up to the point where the sentence was produced. That way, it has to store only the seed value and access count for each sentence, rather than the very bulky tree itself.

There's no limit to how many levels there can be in the syntactical hierarchy of a sentence. (Technically, there's a limit imposed by the size of the program's stack in memory, which can get overfilled by a recursive function.) There is a practical limit on how big the template can be (though it could be expanded if necessary). With the grammars I've used, about sixty items are the most that ever show up in the template. A sixty-word sentence is unusual, though far from a record. (Writing a clear sentence of one hundred words is a good exercise.)

Randomness comes in again when the program takes its finished template off to the dictionary and asks for a particular noun or conjunction or possessive pronoun. From one single template, therefore, the program might produce thousands of different sentences.

And from one brief grammar (the one I used had well under a hundred rules) it can produce thousands of different templates. There's no worry about Prose repeating itself.

Often the words can't be used just as they come from the dictionary. If the sentence calls for a plural noun, for instance, it's easier to make the randomly chosen noun plural than to keep going back to the list over and over until a plural noun happens to turn up. Easier — but not always easy enough. *Car* is simple to pluralize. *City* and *tax* are harder. *Child* is impossible to pluralize by rule, so *children* is in the dictionary.

It would be especially inefficient to store all the different forms of each verb. The tree I've shown here calls for a transitive verb. But "TransVerb" isn't one of the categories in Prose's dictionary. Instead, the program fetches a transitive *infinitive* at random, such as *hoodwink*. Then, taking into consideration the tense, person, and number that may have been established by earlier events in the sentence, it makes the appropriate form of that infinitive: *hookwinked* or *hoodwinks* or *hoodwinking*.

By now it should be no surprise that Prose will produce on demand a large number of very foolish sentences. But to give it its due, it does a couple of things right. First, though some of its products seem quite strange, they are all grammatically correct, with all the urging toward sense that that implies. Second, as I've indicated, it can crank out an enormous *variety* of sentences, of any degree of complexity you care to tell it about in the grammar. The program's main virtue is its flexibility. If you don't like the kinds of sentences it makes, you can change the rules it uses just by editing its grammar file, without having to change the program itself.

Of course there are limits to this flexibility. The program embodies many assumptions about English parts of speech. It would never work with Hebrew or Hopi. As another example, I've distinguished between Nouns and Substances. There are several operational differences, but the simplest is that a Substance is a noun that's often not preceded by an article. *Tree* is a noun, *bark* is a substance. We say "an artichoke" but not "a steam," "speed kills" but "the speeder kills."

This syntactical distinction gets tangled up in semantic ones. We say "I like beef" but not "I like cow." "I like flounder" runs both ways.

The grammar I used is merely one working version. It stresses questions because I've found that they have an especially evocative effect on the reader. (Ron Silliman explored this effect in "Sunset Debris.") There are no rules that use relative pronouns, though there are relative pronouns in the dictionary. Any page of any book will provide many examples of kinds of sentences that prose can't produce because I haven't given it the rules. But it's flexible.

The same applies to the dictionary. The five thousand or so words in the present version (perhaps a quarter of them duplicates or near-duplicates for various purposes) are the result of a long evolution.

The original dictionary of five thousand common words that I gleaned from the word-frequency list for Natural Selection and Auto-Poet turned out to have important flaws. Careful autopsy shows that AutoPoet's terminal boredom was partly due directly to vocabulary. After all, we need to remember where Kuçera and Searle got their corpus of a million words. Much of the English prose they sampled was recent journalism. Some of the material was literary—that is, insistently linguistically interesting. But that material constituted the same small proportion as literature does in the daily use of language. Its effects were swamped just as thoroughly as literature is in the world of printed words. Certainly among the most frequent five thousand words (out of over thirty thousand different words in the million-word corpus), not much was likely to crop up that would testify to the poetry inherent in the American soul. Most of what AutoPoet said sounded as though it came out of a committee.

So I cut words that felt like irredeemable bureaucratese: *accordance, recommendation, facilities, nonspecific, marketing.* In general, any words that pushed a sentence too hard toward abstractness were better omitted: *personality, negative, growth, velocity, location, intervention,* and dozens of others ending with -tion. But also, inappropriately concrete words had to go, such as most names. "Dave" and "Orleans" are among that first five thousand, but they don't help the reader's sense of *focus* in random prose. They're just disorienting.

Some good words, especially verbs, have especially tricky syntactical implications and were best quietly omitted. *Urge* requires a complicated object ("urge A to do B"). Many verbs (*admit, prove, insist*) take a "that" construction, which isn't simple to put into the grammar. *Alike* is usually the complement of a plural copula ("the brothers are alike"); to use it I would have to build in special flags that would keep that whole construction "in mind" until completed. So I dumped those.

Cutting this way brought the list down to a thousand. Then I added words I hoped would have positive effects on a reader's sense of coherence or purpose in the sentences. I began with concrete nouns: *elephant, Bebop, calico, muffin, pewter, clarinet, oak.* Earlier I had gathered for other purposes a special lexicon of words derived from poems I was working on. Many of these words—*checkmate, Babbage, metabolism, Turing, computation*—would serve.

If, as Coleridge said, "poetry is the best words in the best order," then the poet must be a specialist in recognizing "the best words." The pleasure I took in this part of the work was related to the pleasures of poetry. "Best," as sly old Coleridge knew, is a tricky and contingent measure.

Finally, I ran down a list of words I'd gotten from a researcher at Kurzweil Applied Intelligence (KAI) while I worked there as a technical writer. KAI is a major company working on the problem of speech recognition. The words are ones that present special challenges to an automatic recognizer, and the whole group of about two hundred covers the field of English phonemes very thoroughly. Like any set of words chosen for their sound, they form a workable poetic diction. Many sentences that Prose produced benefited from *asterisk, gung-ho, weed, typhoid, sleuth,* and a few dozen others.

There was a question of how many words to add. The obvious way to imitate human speech is to duplicate human vocabulary, but that was just the ground on which AutoPoet had notably failed. The opposite extreme had been used by very early computer poetry experimenters. As *Time* reported (May 25, 1962) about the Auto-Beatnik project, "By drastically cutting down [the program's] choice of words—so that the incidence of a subject word reappearing is greatly increased—engineers can make the machine seem to keep to one topic." (Hugh Kenner used this item from *Time* as the epigraph to his essay, "Art in a Closed Field," published in *Virginia Quarterly Review* late the same year.) But this kind of single-mindedness soon comes to seem merely obsessive—human, but irritating. It was a little like the old Basic English project, six hundred words that would give the third world a common English pidgin. That wasn't what I wanted. I found that a reasonably balanced dictionary of one to two thousand words worked all right, and one of about five thousand gave a pleasant breadth.

Now I had my program; but what to do with it? The first thing I tried was the easiest. I let it run for a while and then combed through the output looking for interesting chunks I could string together. But this approach held onto a residue of my earlier false assumption. I was still treating the computer as a retarded or psychotic human brain from which I could hope for flashes (however far apart) of ordinary or extraordinary lucidity.

At first I saw no alternative. For days, sitting on the train commuting to and from classes, I kept poring over fanfolded piles of computer paper, searching in vain for oracular truths. Jorge Luis Borges has described just this situation in his story "The Library of Babel." He imagines a library of innumerable books of a certain length filled with all the random combinations of letters, in identical rooms stretching toward infinity in all directions. The narrator of the story remembers someone once finding, amid all the megatons of garbage, the phrase "O time thy pyramids." This discovery was a shining moment in the library's dreary, endless history. I was far better off. My dictionary and grammar excluded all but a tiny fraction of the possible combinations. But a tiny fraction of infinity is still infinity; and if "infinity" isn't technically involved (there are only so many possibilities), it might as well be.

Yet there were endless tempting sentences, perhaps one in five or ten: "The court of color (radiation of the center) is stress above any building." Nonsense, yes, but with the subliminal promise of an image: open air, surrounding white buildings, uncanny color. Take out "stress," which is abstract in this context. Notice that "color" makes "radiation" unnecessary (though the connection between them may have first called my attention to "color"). And "court" (as in "courtyard") might contain the implications of both "center" and "building" and made those words unnecessary. So "The court of color is . . ." what? Air, really, or all the air considered as a whole: "atmosphere." "Atmosphere" might also be the courtroom of colors, judiciously discriminating near from far (as in aerial perspective), bright from dim.

But "atmosphere" could never have been produced by the program, not being in its dictionary. *So*, came the subversive voice, *add it to the dictionary.* I was as determined not to cheat as when I selected Travesty outputs for "Monologues of Soul and Body." But I was getting sneakier, too.

So began my work on the second poem reprinted in the Appendix. What I discovered was that I could reverse the process of "Monologues." Instead of feeding my poetry to the computer to digest (or indigest), I could alter its impromptu output to suit my own poetic sense. And what I was doing while I edited this text—the way I could hear myself thinking—felt very much like the way I think when writing poems. Most of any writing process is actually rewriting. Many writers find that the first draft is almost useless in itself. It contains just enough of truth to make the final work, however difficult, possible.

Prose, then, could be treated as a first-draft writer. Many sentences had to be ejected outright. "How was language under volume of the hotel leaving?" presented no foothold to my imagination. "I was evening of the school" didn't set any bells resonating when I came across it. A few sentences slipped through unaltered: "Where is this theory walking?" Others needed only the slightest touch. "Any spirit near man: a town" became "Any spirit near man likes a town," which among other things seems true. (Once again, I was changing the sentence only to something the program *could* have produced.) I found myself on unexpectedly firm ground. All I had to do as editor was to give the outpost a good shake until it settled into place as sense—and keep my ears open for that sense.

So this random output—

> The court of color (radiation of the center) is stress above any building. Light inside the spring marched, but I am place of the science. Since metabolism is typing me, the oak throughout brick has worked. A party up steel: the shot of time. What is a church increasing? Before I have made us, the voice of woman (a dark dark) was numbering earth, and an easy sea does.

—rather quickly became this language I felt I could stand behind:

> The court of color is atmosphere. Light in the spring marches, but place is the true science. While metabolism types us, the oak has worked through brick, and the breath knows ghosts. Before creation, the voice of woman (a dark dark) was numbering earth, as an easy sea does.

I liked the historical sweep, the balance between nostalgia and admonition, the modulation from one metaphor to the next. Versions of light ("color" and "spring," and "a dark dark") mingle with opaque solidities like "oak," "brick," "earth," maybe "place." The slow "oak" inexorably forcing its way "through brick" stands against the faster "breath" and "voice" and "march" of the light. Yet everything is changing and alive, merely exhibiting different "types" of "metabolism." Linking all the images is the "sea," both restless and "easy," clear and dark, inanimate yet sentient enough to "number" the "earth" it washes, grain by grain.

One interesting point in the final version is the addition of "and the breath knows ghosts." I wrote that, not the program. Yet it's not a phrase I could imagine myself finding, except under the spell of the program's language, so dreamily detached from the immediate necessities of saying things. But each breath we take includes atoms breathed by Bach and Caligula. If the breath doesn't know ghosts, what does it know?

Several questions lingered, nagging. *Was* this fiddling with the computer's output really cheating? And if coherent meaning suffused "paragraphs" like this, who was making it? Is the paraphrase I spelled out a moment ago due to the poet or to an overingenious critic?

Yet these questions finally answered each other. I wasn't doing artificial intelligence research but writing poems. And I wasn't trying to imitate a human poet. The point of my work wasn't the power or originality of the program itself. (Later I discovered—with no surprise—that about the same time I was writing Prose, Chris Westbury, in Montreal, was producing the freeware program McPoet, which seems to use the same familiar principles of a "context-free grammar.") The point, rather, was seeing how to use what it could do.

I was taking seriously the lesson I found in some of the most intriguing poetry of the present time: to let the play of language stand on the stage of the page in its own ordinary mysteriousness, encouraging the reader not just to participate in making sense but to be conscious of participating. I'd been preparing for some time (as a critic, as a reader, as a poet) to write in a new way. Several decades of thinking about poetry taught me what to ask from the computer. And the stimulus of those random sentences, in turn, brought home the possibilities I'd glimpsed. My programming and my poetry writing were at last teaching each other.

The criteria for *sense* that my ear set in the course of (re)writing would become the reader's necessary criteria, too. And that, I had come to realize, is how the writing of any poetry works. The poet sets the rules that stake out a territory in the endless realm of language, trying not to go so far out as to lose the reader's natural trust. As readers, we revel in our meaning-making ingenuity. This makes us want to trust the poem. As Wallace Stevens put it, "Poetry must resist the intelligence almost successfully." I had always known this, but the experiments were bringing the point home with a new directness.

I kept collecting and editing sentences until I knew (though it would be hard to say how) that I had enough. What next? How to make a poem out of sentences? I toyed with the idea of lineating them, turning them into verse, but then decided that prose was their right form after all. Yet I didn't want one huge unreadable block. So I began looking for joints in this body.

These points of articulation give the whole thing a shape. They make it possible to say, for instance, that the poem has fourteen parts. (Does the fourteen-line shape of the sonnet have an influence here?) Even this simple division gives the text a useful kind of structure. A reader can see relations among 14 sections more easily than among 139 sentences.

Also, every break between sections is a place for both starting and stopping. If these two sentences are run together,

> Unless I had planned you, I would ask, How are the voices increasing? I am thinking this.

then "this" in the second sentence simply refers to the first sentence. But when the two are divided by a break between sections (II and III), "this" refers more to the whole poem. The break also emphasizes the link between the "you" in the first sentence and the explicit and implicit elements of address in previous sentences of section II. Addressing a "you" becomes part of what that section is *about*, part of its pattern of gestures.

One of the sentences worked equally well as a beginning point and an ending point. The one before it was a good ending, and the one after was another good beginning. The result was a one-sentence section:

X

> I was meaning to filter out meaning from the paper, but form—a heart—had charged something.

So isolated, the sentence becomes a comment on the project of the poem itself. It points to a kind of miracle in how a text begets an activity. In the first clause, "filter" and "paper" emphasize the mechanical operations of written language. "Paper" also suggests newspapers, the "white papers" of diplomats, and the dutiful "papers" of students, as well as the medium of print itself. "Meaning," repeated this way, is reduced to mere willful busyness. (T. S. Eliot once said that "meaning" in poetry is the piece of meat that the burglar throws to the dog; it keeps the forebrain quiet while the poem does its real work.) The second clause answers with two metaphors: a "heart" that gives both physical and emotional life and the "charge" of what Whitman called "the body electric." These metaphors donate their force to "form," which once meant *beauty* or *arrangement* or the *wholeness* that makes anything a thing at all ("something"). "Form" is this section's word for how words rise up to become part of us. The sequence of verb tenses says that this essential activity of language was going on behind my back, even while I was trying to do something less.

It feels more accurate to say that I found these dividing points than to say that I created them. I discovered the poem's form within it. All that remained was to find a title. I wanted to emphasize what the poem was made of and the points where imagination was called on to fill the gaps of juxtaposition: the sentences and the boundaries between them. When I inventoried the poem, I found that it contained seventy-six assertions and sixty-three questions, and that's what I called it.

AVENUES

"Seventy-Six Assertions and Sixty-Three Questions" was a new kind of poem for me, not only in its computer origin but in its style and sound. In its way, the computer was collaborating now. It was helping me think about poetry. Not simply confirming or codifying knowledge I already had, like the chorale-harmonization program, it was becoming a tool of discovery.

I kept exploring the possibilities of Prose. One of the simplest variations arose through an outside request. Every other year, Connecticut College's Center for Arts and Technology hosts a symposium, and at one of these I gave a brief talk about Prose. Afterward, Manfred Fischbeck, choreographer and teacher at the University of the Arts in Philadelphia, approached me to ask whether the dictionary that Prose used could be changed. I said yes, that I'd designed it that way on purpose. He told me about a new piece he was working on, involving dancers and film and music and words. We agreed on this: He would sit down with his dancers and get them to list words—nouns, verbs, and adjectives—associated with dance and with this project. I would make a new dictionary, keeping all the necessary "linguistic glue" words like conjunctions and pronouns but replacing the usual long lists of referential words with the relatively short lists of words the dancers chose. Then I would generate text and edit from it about two minutes' worth of sentences to be spoken (by Manfred) as a voiceover during the first section of the dance. The result is printed in the appendix as "Dance Text." Here's the opening:

The stage reverses a closed room, where every rehearsal draws
    its unreal distance.

Repetition: the machine of memory.
Turbulence: a traveling repetition.
The reward of turbulence: balance.
Performance is language, but we think to feel.
To think is the beginning of work.
To imagine gives speed.
To fall is slowing down, and to accelerate is any jump.
Space becomes the page of dance, where we flow between the
    dream and the blue beat.
Deep time: so dark a figure.
Someone is a shape.
When we were these many gestures, you were these many colors.
While all the dancers are bending these rhythms, the cloud of
    hands calls the ballet across the face of the air.
To talk is a dimension; to organize is music.
The mechanics of dream connect these nerves in groups.

This was still editing normal Prose output. But I'd also been trying out different attitudes toward computer-generated text. One idea, always in the back of my mind, treated the computer's language as *oracular*. I was thinking partly of the Greek oracles—a word that means both the representatives of the gods to whom people took important questions and the puzzling truths with which they answered. The oracles usually turned out to be truthful in ways nobody understood until it was too late. Greeks from Oedipus through Euclid believed fervently in the truth but were fatalistic about its usefulness. Most human cultures seem to prize anonymous, cryptic statements embodying wisdom. Proverbs are another form of oracle. They can be very mysterious. Barbara Herrnstein Smith, a critic who has thought about proverbs as a special kind of literature, likes this German one: "When the wind blows, the tree shakes." There's almost nothing it can't refer to, no situation in which it *doesn't* offer prudent advice. It's up to us to interpret it correctly for each occasion. You could clear your throat at a tense moment in any meeting, utter that sentence, and sit back, confident in your reputation for insight.

This recalls the play between sense and nonsense we examined earlier. It may also bring us back to randomness. One kind of oracle used in the Middle Ages was the *sortes Virgilianae*; when you had a problem, you would open Virgil's *Aeneid* at random, point blindly to a line, and then read it as a commentary on your question. It's the same principle as in the *I Ching*. *Sortes* means "lots" (as in "casting lots") and finally comes to mean "fate" or "destiny". There's an old link between chance and necessity; both are names for what's outside our control.

Some cultures take their wisdom as it comes, some collect it in memory, and some even write it down. Then it becomes "scripture," which means "writing" but especially (while writing is a new and rare skill) holy writing, the transcribed word of a god or God. A few cultures go on to add layers of interpretation and commentary to this basic scripture. The Hindus are a good example. But no one has outdone the Jews in this respect. The clearest monument to this is the Talmud.

I'm no expert on the Talmud, but the outlines of its history are readily accessible. Moses brought down from Mount Sinai two laws: the Ten Commandments written on stone and a body of oral law that each generation of priests must teach to the next. This oral law, the *halakhah*, together with the oral commentary that grew up around it, became known as the Mishnah. During the five centuries between the destruction of the Temple and the destruction of the Roman Empire, the Mishnah was written down; and an enormous mass of further commentary, called the Gemara, began to be built on top of it. Relevant quotations from the Torah were added for confirmation and resolution of obscure points. Important commentaries by later rabbis also attached themselves to the Mishnah and Gemara. The whole thing became known as the Talmud, from a root word that means *learning*.

A page in a fine Talmud is visually striking. At the top of the page, in heavy Hebrew print, is a small rectangle of the Mishnaic text. Surrounding it on the bottom and both sides, in lighter type, is the long Gemara for that part of the Mishnah. There are many pages in each of many volumes. An old saying equates the Talmud with an ocean that a lifetime would barely suffice to swim across.

I began to think of imitating, from that enormous work, a principle of construction, a way to both invoke and modify people's normal poetry-reading reflexes. Taking output from Prose as my "Mishnah," my text for commentary, I could write something modeled on the Talmud. Of course the idea wasn't to comment on the Talmud itself. I wouldn't be likely to call my poem "A Talmud" or to quote from that masterwork of many authors. I wouldn't even treat similar topics. All I wanted was a design.

The great appeal of the Talmud's method is that it's so mutlivocal. There are voices upon voices upon voices: the *halakhah*; the prescriptural oral commentaries on it in the Mishnah; the anonymous original layers of the Gemara (collected by hundreds of teachers over hundreds of years); the further notes and clarifications and stories added by later, named rabbis; the references to the books of the Torah. Any section of the Talmud resounds with many personalities, no matter how intently they all focus on a single, minutely defined topic, such as the proper treatment of stones found underneath a tree that is worshipped by heathens.

Imitating this kind of communal work wouldn't be completely off the poetic track historically. The impulse toward multiple voices has informed a lot of modern poetry. The literary theorist Mikhail Bakhtin distinguished lyric poetry, which he called *monologic*, from the *dialogic* nature of novels. A novel echoes not just with the words of different characters but with the languages of different classes, professions, age groups, cliques, clans, and parties. Yet poetry, too, can be dialogic. In a sense, how could it not be? Our own selves aren't simple, single entities. As Bakhtin says, "The ideological becoming of a human being . . . is the process of selectively assimilating the words of others." Eliot's *Waste Land* and Pound's *Cantos* and Williams's *Paterson* in their various ways juxtaposed not only images but voices. This impulse has deepened in recent decades, whether in John Ashbery's strongly mixed diction or in Jerome Rothenberg's adaptations of tribal communions. For any poet who has grown dissatisfied with the monologic lyric voice, the Talmud might offer an intriguing model.

What could the voices of such a poem be? However disparate their origins, the computer's random prose, like the arcane Mishnah, seems to call for commentary. How would I go about supplying interpretation for it? Of course, I would rely on my own experience as a reader. But "I"—not only as a reader with an education and a history of my own but as a self created partly by dialogic interchange with the world around me—have potentially many voices.

For instance, what does a careful reader do when something isn't clear? Faced with the problem of interpreting an obscure text, one of my first impulses is to look up certain words in the dictionary. (How do I know which ones to look up?) The Torah is most often used in the Gemara for just the purpose—to establish the correct meaning of particular words. But the dictionary, too, is a kind of scripture. It's an anonymous systemization of all the essentials of human life. In argument or in Scrabble, we frequently appeal to its supreme authority. We say "the Dictionary"—though there are many dictionaries— much as we say "the Bible," which means "book." Furthermore, as a literary scholar, in a critical pinch I don't use just any dictionary. I turn to the *Oxford English Dictionary*, the fattest and most authoritative of all. The OED's authority is itself dialogic, derived from the masses of quotations that bring into this one book the whole history of our literary culture.

Even without the dictionary, within my own private response to certain evocative sentences that emerge from the Prose machine, I can hear more than one character speaking. There's a finicky analyst of logic and grammar; a fellow who luxuriates in images conjured up (however remotely) by any fragment of phrase; a literary interpreter of figures of speech, and so on. I began to see a rare opportunity to work simultaneously as poet and as critic. The layers piled up before my eyes.

Getting the text to comment on would mean going back a step. Treating the Prose output as oracular involves treating it as quasi-sacred—it wouldn't be appropriate to edit it. So it was back to scouting through reams of random text, looking for nuggets of wisdom. As compared with the weary seeker of AutoPoet days, I would need only single sentences, not stretches where meter and syntax combine to make plausible poetry.

This experiment grew logically out of "Seventy-Six Assertions and Sixty-Three Questions," even though the model I was starting from was quite different. In both cases, the computer program offered text, and I offered interpretation. In the earlier poem, the interpretation was superimposed on the text as editing. In the newer experiment, the interpretation was added after the text and surrounded it without covering it up.

I'll give just one example: a sentence I found in a pile of Prose, and the commentary I built up around it:

WHAT CANNOT THE GLASS OF AIR HURT? Glass clear as air lends air also frangibility. (The sparrow, deceived, died.) Thus shards; and the hurt at the heart of all flesh figures as laceration. And the same transparency that speaks of air breaking presents that glass which aids long vision, or close vision, the pain the pain that attends sight.[1] And the sand-glass—behold, "her glasse is runne," shards raining around naked feet are shards of time. Not "Whom" but "What"; for *time that bears all things digests all things, and not persons only.*[2] Is there a glint among these cinders? The word is "cannot," rather than the indicative "does not" or the minatory "will not"; does this suggest an option, the hurt nullified or evaded, the glass able but unwilling to wound? so that the poet has said, "Sweet, it hurts not"?

---

1. Likewise, the glass is a burning glass, vision a fire to the eye. And the looking glass, most treacherous of all.
2. And this word "What" echoes the sound of universal termination, which Babhli heard whispered on the breeze on the side of the mountain; beginning in aspiration (which the Anglo-Saxons rightly placed first in their orthographies, *hwat*), running through that brusque vocable/vowel, clapped shut between palate and tongue, the secret.

Trial passages like this one never came together into a finished work for me. But the method fed into a more recent long-term project, a kind of personal encyclopedia of one-page definitions of (the project says) everything under the sun. (It's called *Except to Be*, partly because its prose never uses any form of the verb *to be*.) The impulse behind that entirely noncomputer work evolved, at least in part, from my thinking about the computer-based experiment.

What's next? The obvious lack in Prose is semantics. At its cleverest, the program is still never talking *about* anything. I've suggested

how language in poetry works in other important ways besides re-
ferring to or signifying things. But most poetry also refers to things in
the normal way as well. To do that, a generator of language (person
or program) has to know something about things as well as about
syntax.

As a crude beginning I could add another set of tags to each word
in the dictionary, indicating a set of "topics" to which the word is
relevant. This seems to be the approach of Racter in *The Policeman's Beard
Is Half-Constructed*, which I described in the Introduction. According to
A. K. Dewdney, Racter works with sentence templates like this: "THE
noun.an verb.3p.et THE noun.fd." "An," "et," and "fd" mean "ani-
mal, "eating," and "food," respectively. These identifiers are at-
tached to selected words in the dictionary, so the program seeking a
"noun.an" selects only from words with the ".an" tag. If the pro-
grammer builds in a tendency for the same tags to keep turning up in
several sentences, the program will seem to stick to a topic.

Yet for general-purpose meaning making, this wouldn't be very
promising. Who defines a "topic"? *Roget's Theasaurus* contains a "Syn-
opsis of Categories" that places all the possible things to talk about in
an orderly outline. That could be a starting point. But if you're stuck
with Peter Roget's idea of how the world is divided up, it becomes
difficult to say anything interesting—at least by chance.

What's required is a kind of road map of the semantic "space"
through which we move when we're talking. But it's a "space" in far
more dimensions than three, and sometimes it seems to change even
while we're traversing it. Analyzing this and codifying it in a com-
puter program is a job for legions of programmers. In fact, here we
are in the true realm of artificial intelligence, where, for now at least,
the experts will have to take over. Even they haven't yet had any
overwhelming success, though they seem to be getting closer.

In any case, this is the Imitation Game again. The trap for poetry is
that the more accurately the computer mimics human language,
the more ordinary it becomes. In fact, the ordinariness is how we
measure the accuracy of imitation. The perfect AI language machine
would convince us (win the Turing game) by being rather dull, like a

good secret agent. The computer poet wants a more unstable balance of the plain and the strange.

Partly because I was running up against a taller mountain than I had much interest in climbing, I began to think again about the other main approach to "computer poetry": not text generation but text manipulation. These are the two logical choices, which you could diagram as.

PROGRAM ———————> TEXT

and

TEXT ————> PROGRAM————> TEXT

A program like Prose generates new text without any input; a program like Travesty transforms one text into another. The number of possible transformations must be huge, and I began looking for interesting ones.

One method came to my attention through a delightful book by Jackson Mac Low called *The Virginia Woolf Poems* (Burning Deck Press, 1986). In an endnote to the book, Jackson explained the "diastic" or "spelling-thru" technique he had used in writing the poems. The process began with a striking phrase from Virginia Woolf's *The Waves*: "ridiculous in Picadilly." He reread the novel, looking for the first word that, like "ridiculous," began with an r; then the next word following that had (like "ridiculous") i as its second letter; then the next whose third letter was d; and so on until he had "spelled through" the whole phrase. (There were other rules for line breaks, punctuation, and so on.) The resulting text would be made entirely out of Woolf's words but would have none of the usual English syntax. As I read the poems, I was startled by how evocative a text this arbitrary system could produce.

Jackson had done all his work by hand. I sat down and embodied his rules in a little program called Diastext. I sent it to him, and he has used it in the making of several books since.

I also sent it to Hugh Kenner, the author of Travesty. Probably at the same time, I sent him a computer-disk copy of a wonderful "text" I had found, a little pamphlet called *Sentences for Analysis and Parsing*, from the Thayer Street Grammar School in Providence, Rhode Island. (It's anonymous, and what may be the only copy sits in a modest folder in the Brown University library. I tracked down Samuel Stillman Greene, a mid-nineteenth-century Providence educator, as the probable author.) The little book consists of 457 sentences, ranging from "Dogs barked" and "Halt!" through grandiose entries like "He spoke in as noble accents as ever fell from human lips." I had already used the text in one peculiar, if noncomputer, way, writing a one-act play called *Beauties*, for four characters, all of whose dialogue is made up of sentences from the pamphlet.

It was Hugh's idea to run the schoolbook text first through his Travesty program a number of times and then to run those outputs through Diastext in turn. Using the same sort of diagram as before, we could see this as

TEXT ——> PROGRAM ——> TEXT ——> PROGRAM ——> TEXT

We sorted through a good many of the results (each of them a Travesty output followed by the diastic "spelling through" of that output), picked the ones we liked, and put titles on them. The result is a book called *Sentences*, which Sun & Moon (a California press largely devoted to the work of "language" poets) published in 1995. (It displays, as Hugh notes in the Afterword, "an odd fixation on cigars.") One section (too long to insert here) appears in the Appendix.

Jackson's "diastic" method of text manipulation is arbitrary, not random. The process is completely deterministic once the author has chosen the input text (*The Waves*) and the "seed" phrase ("ridiculous in Picadilly"). You could even eliminate the seed phrase by making the text itself its own seed. (With a big input text, this produces a really enormous output; but you could—arbitrarily—cut it off at some point.) Turning that into a program is very straightforward, because the method is already an algorithm.

This got me thinking about other arbitrary linguistic algorithms, and I remembered a very old one: the Cabalists had various systems for translating letters into numbers and determining the mystic significance of words by way of the numbers their letters added up to. Some of these systems were very complicated, but one is about the simplest imaginable: $A = 1$, $B = 2$, and so on. So the word *word* totals 60; *abracadabra* is 52.

If I didn't want to construct a system of mystic significances, what could I do with these numbers? I noticed that while every word has a unique total, each total corresponds to several or many words; how many depends roughly on how large the number is. Huge arrays of words cluster around values between about 20 and 100. Coincidences diminish above 100 and become sparser and sparser as the totals rise. This numerology, in other words, can be seen not as characterizing single words but as identifying *groups* of words. Well, poems—from a certain peculiar point of view—consist of groups of words.

I wrote a tiny program, Numerol, that would read an input text, then ask the user repeatedly for a number, and write out all the words in the text with that total. As a refinement, I had the program use the *modulus* of the number, so the program wrote out all words whose total was evenly divisible by user's number. In practice, this didn't make much difference; it just intensified the clustering of words around lower values. In any case I found the results most interesting when I gave the program numbers in the range between 100 and 150.

As input, I used a file containing the complete manuscript of a book of poems I was working on. This didn't just establish some more formal "authorship" for me in the output; in my own eyes at least, it put my unmistakable stamp on the results. Especially in the range of those higher totals, we're talking about words outside the realm of the inevitable: not *because* and *tree* and *that* but *improvised* and *Plymouth* and *fingerbowls*. Those three words all total 130, and each of them is a word with which I have strong personal associations. The groups of words the program offered me felt like a collection of mirrors.

These personal associations are—well, personal. A handful of three or four words might have private meaning but would make collective sense to someone else only by accident. On the other hand, a collection of these collections of words begins to build up a picture, visible even from the outside, of a person, at least as a bundle of obsessions and habits and linguistic quirks. I had chosen the words in writing the poems; the program gave me a way to examine those acts

of choice and present them *as* acts of choice. After looking over doz-
ens of groups, I selected the ones that felt more telling and treated
each one as a section within a poem.

The words in each group have no syntactical relation to each
other, of course. This suggested that I should present them as collec-
tions and not so much as *sequences* (like the words in a sentence or even
a line). Poetry in this century has already developed techniques for
treating words that way. They involve using the two-dimensional
space on the page, undermining the one-dimensional sequence by
which printed language usually imitates the stream of syntactical
speech. So more of my own choice entered as I arranged the words
on the page. Here's one section from the middle of the poem:

consequence

yourself,

everybody

thousands.   yourself.

shattering yourself

alternating twisting pressure

thousands

dissipates yourself

versions   tortured,

convenient

Finally, I selected one two-word group as my title, "Extraordinary
Instruments." (Each word totals 172.) It's one of the few groups that

happens to offer a coherent *phrase*; and the phrase resonated with my feeling, in looking through all these selections from a personal dictionary or code book I had hardly known I kept, of how powerfully single words identify a way of looking at the world. I wasn't sure whether the "instruments" were musical or surgical, but at this level of linguistic abstraction I wasn't even sure of the difference.

Later, a logical alternative to this method occurred to me. By using my own other poems as the source text, I had predetermined the diction of "Extraordinary Instruments," and part of the poem's effect was to explore that diction. (It's a pretty narcissistic poem, in an obscure way.) From an odd angle, I was secretly reviving the old idea of a "poetic diction"—a set of words proper for use in poetry. Rebellions against this idea, whether Wordsworth's or Pound's, have had two motives in various proportions: to expand the range of poetry and to democratize it. Why not, in the spirit of perversity, take this principle all the way and give *every* word an equal chance?

I hunted around for a text-only online dictionary of English and found one with over a hundred thousand words—barely ten or twenty per cent of English but a respectable vocabulary for a college graduate. Then I built a new filter program, much like Numerol, that would accept a number from the user and report back every word in the dictionary whose letters summed to that number. The lists were long, especially for numbers under 100. Instead of receiving from the program a little handful of words to arrange in a section, I could get a sizable vocabulary out of which to build a poem. The obvious rule was that, whatever number I chose, the resulting poem couldn't contain any words not in the list.

Running through my head for days, like an ad jingle, had been the phrase "That's glory," which I thought was Dylan Thomas or Samuel Beckett until I realized it was Humpty Dumpty. ("There's glory for you!" is how he gets into explaining that he pays words extra to mean what he wants.) The total for *that's* is 68; the apostrophe doesn't count. The list of 68-words, about a thousand of them, included some splendid collisions: *goofy* and *logos, diligence* and *swank* and so on. The challenge of building a coherent poem out of these—without the help of *the* (33) or *and* (19) or *a* (1)—wasn't one in which the computer could help me much. But working from the computer's list, I could know I wasn't letting a foreign word slip in:

> That's acceptable. That's goofy
> elating language: gleeful logos
> nobly jeering, lauding drily—
> that's doings. That's bagsful,
> that's unabated beauts. That's
> poems readably suave, trued,
> pleading diligence, calving jetsam,
> dangling acuter Damoclean dangers
> safely. That's swank. . . .

Naturally enough, the poem turned out to be about poems and the various kinds of talking they could do.

Once again, the advantage of the computer here lies in its perfect ignorance of language as such. The necessities of evolution vitally condition and limit our reception and emission of words. We need to survive in social situations where a tendency to hear (like one of Woody Allen's characters) "Did you?" as "Jew?" would at least complicate our lives. (We can afford to mishear songs, and we do; my friend Preston McClanahan thought it went, "For he's a jolly good fellow, / with so many candy knives.") Computers fail to acknowledge the probabilities of human talk, which gives the designers of speech-recognition machines nightmares. But by the same token, humans may find it hard to play as freely in the field of language as poetry invites.

How many random or arbitrary methods for manipulating or selecting language could there be? Infinitely many? And of those, how many are potentially interesting? If there are answers to these questions, we'll find hints of them only through a very large number of experiments. As a poet trained in the use of traditional forms— though I use them only intermittently—I saw a connection between the long history of exploration that has given us those forms and the kinds of experiments encouraged by the search for text manipulation.

A new form begins as someone's invention and then, maybe,

proves useful to other poets. We know one Greek form as the "Sapphic stanza." It may have been worked out originally by her contemporary, Alcaeus, but it was a favorite of Sappho's, and she used it in writing some magnificent poems. We still give it her name, though for thousands of years poets from Catullus through James Merrill have been using it—and varying it. The differences between Greek and a language like English *require* some variations. (In the pattern that defines the form, we usually replace "quantity," or syllable duration, with stress.) It has a distinctive shape on the page, so any more or less regular stanza that more or less resembles it is likely to register as a variation on the Sapphic stanza. These variations in a form can work like mutations in biology, providing the material for evolution. Ezra Pound claimed that the sonnet began as someone's variation on the older canzone.

Will certain computer poetry methods catch on and establish themselves and evolve in similar ways? Or will we shift the demand for originality in poems toward meta-originality in method? Another decade or two should tell us.

I'll close with one more example. Talking about "deterministic" systems these days is likely to bring up the fashionable subject of chaos. "Chaos" is our name for the way a simple, deterministic system can turn out to have unpredictable results. The weather, for instance, is the result of physical laws—gravity, friction, thermal expansion—that every high school physics student knows. But a radio station that gives a thousand-dollar "guarantee" on its forecast for the day's high temperature, even when the guarantee is only for accuracy within five degrees either way, pays out a thousand dollars two or three times a month.

Many formulas are known by now that produce chaos when key variables approach some particular value. One of them, an "iterative function" that can be used to model population growth, looks like this:

$$r*p*(1 - p) \longrightarrow p.$$

It becomes "chaotic" as r approaches 4. (It turns out that r can never reach 4; the equation explodes infinitely at that point.) Suppose we use this formula to select, over and over, from a little collection of twelve or fifteen worlds? We write the program, give it the little pile of words, and start plugging in values for r. At low values the results are infinitely repetitious and therefore boring—but sometimes *intrestingly* boring if we put them into the right context. The simplest context is a series, in which we can see the results growing more and more complex as r increases. As with increasing values of n in Travesty, something seems to be struggling toward coherence. It would be whimsical, but logical, to end the sequence with a section that uses the words to make perfectly good sense and call it "r = 4.0"—as if "perfectly good sense" were the result of chaos gone ballistic. One result is given in the Appendix, a poem called "And Finger Light Because Almost Finger Elsewhere." (The title phrase occurs in one of the results I didn't finally use.) A different group of words and different values for r would produce infinitely many different poems.

UNCONCLUSION

I don't think computer poetry teaches us much about computers, so far. Or at least mine doesn't; as I've said several times, these programs don't push programming into new territory. What I find interesting is that these experiments, which are so simple from a computer science point of view, can help remind us in a new way of things we already knew about poetry and about language.

Maybe this isn't surprising. The originators of the cabalistic system I mentioned in the preceding chapter were almost certainly responding to a new *technology* of language—writing—when they began to treat words as hidden numbers. (Preliterate people, for whom language is exclusively speech, can't think of words as composed of letters that might have numerical equivalents.) Early in the twentieth century, poets, especially Williams and Pound and Charles Olson, discovered new expressive resources in such techniques as the precise two-dimensional arrangement of words on the page, which made poetry a little more like painting. These discoveries depended on a technological innovation: the typewriter. Typewriters took the capabilities that printers had enjoyed for centuries and made them available directly to authors. Williams's extremely careful use of lineation—now part of the toolkit of hundreds of poets—depended on his ability to produce quickly, in his own study, dozens of variations on the "printed" artifact of his poem. Some people argue that computers, simply as word-processing machines, have begun to transform writing too. Probably any technology newly applied to language will suggest a sudden new slant on the words by and among which we live.

Thinking up ways to "do computer poetry" makes us look at language and poetry from an unfamiliar angle. This seems appropriate if one of poetry's functions is to make us aware, with a fresh intensity, of our relation to the language that constitutes so much of human life—or if you like, of how language constitutes so much of our relation to the world. How do words mean when we put them into new contexts? Under what conditions does the meaning web tear apart? What meanings can words make (or can we make of them) when we disturb their normal relation to each other? These are questions that any poet can be seen as asking; and from this point of view, someone experimenting with computer poetry is continuing an age-old project.

One of the first things I relearned from working with programs like Prose was how essential the reader is to the poem. Part of this can be put in simple economic terms: the reader is a consumer, and any manufacturer who ignores the consumer's needs goes out of business. But the point is not, God help us, that poets should anxiously adjust the poem-product to current demand. (As readers we need far more then we may know we need or can think to ask for.) Instead, we're bound to recognize that writing a poem is entering into an elaborate, subtle, unspoken contract with the possible readers of that poem—the kind of contract that binds a family or a society together, not once and for all, but over and over again every day.

So those diagrams I showed in the preceding chapter are seriously incomplete. Whether the computer generates or manipulates text, we need to see it in context:

PROGRAM ————> TEXT ————> READER

or

TEXT ————> PROGRAM ————> TEXT ————> READER

This correction is likely to make us think about poetry in what M. H. Abrams calls "pragmatic" rather than "expressive" terms. That is, rather than dwelling on how the poet has said what the poet wanted to say, we'll probably concentrate on how the reader is affected by the poem. This means asking what the poem *does* and looking at the devices and choices and parts of a poem as the ways it does it. The reader's role isn't just to be a spectator but to be the arena in which the poem acts itself out.

If the reader is so important, we could also think of moving him or her away from that end-of-the-road box in the diagrams and back into the process somewhere. We could try to make the reader's constructive role in the poem more conscious, for instance by giving the reader explicit choices to make. The catchword here is "interactive poetry," and poets have begun exploring several possibilities in this direction. In 1989, a Canadian poet, Rod Willmot, wrote "Everglade," which he calls "the first hypertext poem ever created." Hypertext, a very hot topic these days, is essentially an attempt to make text (which we normally think of as a speechlike, linear string of words) multidimensional. In a way, texts of all kinds have always done this. We remember, we read back and forth, we make connections that couldn't be diagrammed in one dimension. The Talmud, as my colleague Roger Brooks argues, is a hypertext without computer technology. The basic text of the Mishnah is surrounded on the page by the most important links to other texts, and the traditional Talmudic scholar is the living embodiment of a vastly larger network of such links. (The computer, especially the CD-ROM that can place the vast literature of the Talmud within the computer's instantaneous reach, has been a blessing to scholars.)

Willmot's poem is several dozen computer-screen-sized poems. With a click of the mouse, the reader can see one or more words highlighted on the screen. Each of these, with another click, turns out to be a link to another poem. The associative links aren't just coincidences of words; they're part of the poet's meaning—the meaning of the *whole* poem, a meaning *behind* the individual screen of poetry.

Though hypertext is advertised as a kind of apotheosis, as what text always wanted to be when it grew up, in a sense this approach reduces the role of text. The poem itself becomes a *path* through the network of texts. Since there are many paths and since the order in which we read different pieces of a poem affects our sense of what the whole poem means, "Everglade" is many poems. Here again is our old friend the arbitrary, but now it's the reader who exercises it and in that sense participates in the making of the poem. The French poet Raymond Queneau made a work with a similar effect in the precomputer middle of the century. His "Hundred Billion Sonnets" looks like ten perfectly normal sonnets—except that each line in each sonnet can be replaced by the corresponding line in any of the others. His title points out that this allows for 10^{14} different fourteen-line sonnets (a hundred billion). Clearly the reader is expected to construct and read some selection of these (just a selection; if each one takes a minute to read, the complete work would occupy us all day every day for 190 million years).

Enthusiasm for this realm of possibilities shouldn't make us forget, though, that *all* poems are interactive. The reader is always an essential collaborator, if not in the making of the text, still in the making of meaning. We act as careful readers by making choices; the most essential one we make is to read the poem *again*; and each time we do, we read a somewhat different poem. When Robert Frost begins "The Most of It" with the line "He thought he kept the universe alone," we can hear "thought" as emphasized (he was mistaken, maybe foolish, to think so) or not (he was framing a hypothesis, pending further data). We can hear "kept" as a synonym for "preserved" (guarded from intrusion) or for "maintained" (as in *housekeeping*). We can hear "alone" as belonging with the second "he" (he and only he kept the universe) or as an adverb describing his lonely state. Each of these possibilities changes our sense of everything that happens later in the poem. Yet the choices aren't exclusive—we don't settle on one and reject the others—but cumulative. What the poem "means" is the sum of these possibilities and the ways they modify each other. Most readers won't hear all of these on the first time through, so "The Most of It" grows with each rereading.

If the poet lets the reader know that a computer was involved in the making of the poem, then the reader's awareness of interacting with the poem can be oddly heightened. I've remarked before that the presence of computer peculiarities in a poem's language tends to enhance our sense of strangeness—our suspicion of the language, as it were. We're pushed one step back from immediate saying-and-hearing; the language shifts from *use* toward *mention*.

Another way to put it is that the computer's intervention can make the poet and the reader aware (and what poet and reader are aware of constitutes the meaning of the poem) of the peculiar objectivity of language. Language has everything in the world to do with persons and personalities. To a very large extent our personalities, among our fellow humans, are created by and embodied in what we *say*. Furthermore, language is made by people. There's no one else who can do it. Schoolchildren come to think of language as authoritatively enshrined in the anonymous Dictionary; but dictionaries have authors (usually committees of authors), and language has a history. Every word we speak was once spoken for the first time by somebody, and it didn't exist until then. Yet it feels very odd to think of language as being made by people, because we almost never see it happening. Whom do you know who has invented a word, one that entered into the language people speak or write?

Language is what some scientists have taken to calling an "emergent" phenomenon, like a brain or an epidemic or a stock market crash or a culture. Partly this means that you can't get to the meaning of a sentence by adding up the meanings of its individual words. But it also says something about how language arises and grows. We don't see people at work inventing language, but countless unconscious acts of creative variation are going on all around us. A slight change in pronunciation, a slight carelessness in the use of a word that becomes habitual, a plausible stab at reforming an old word to fit a new situation—these things that happen all the time accumulate to change languages and ultimately to make new ones. (Some variations accumulate; most die out.) To repeat a metaphor I used in the preceding chapter to talk about poetic form, these acts are to language what mutations are to biology—the material for evolution; and the evolution's engine is a kind of natural selection that works on this material. This is why a historical family tree of languages looks exactly like the bushy growths that evolutionary biologists draw.

So the language belongs to *all* of us rather than to *any* of us. This rigorous commonality keeps us linguistically honest (more or less). Humpty Dumpty—"I pay words extra, and they mean what I want"—will ultimately cut himself off from language, because a language requires at least two speakers who agree on it. A more intensely focused version of the same commonality keeps us honest in the give-and-take of a poet and reader coconstructing a poem. Students often worry: "But won't everyone read the poem differently? Won't everybody have a different interpretation?" Yes, in one sense, but only in the sense that we're all different. We're also all the same; our genetic makeup, our anatomical construction, even our personal histories are identical to within vanishingly small (if all-important to us) degrees of variation. The language communities to which we belong heavily constrain the interpretations we'll produce for a given bit of text. A poet and a reader make up a tiny community that depends on those larger, containing communities.

It's not just interpretation that's constrained by all this history and circumstance; what we say is also constrained to a great extent. How much of what you said in the course of yesterday consisted of things like "How are you?" and "Pass me the salt, would you?" If that makes for a close and happy community, if it keeps us from circling each other warily like competing species at a water hole, it also threatens to make life dull. If our talk makes our personalities, we'd just as soon find something to say that nobody else would quite say. A job of poetry, again, is to keep refreshing the possibilities for things to be said and heard. Maybe the job of language is to say what the world gives us to say. But it's also true that language, discovering new ways of saying things, generates new things to say. Here the computer can help in some direct if crude ways.

Furthermore, whether the reader knows what was involved in the making of a poem or not, the use of computers objectifies some aspects of the writing of poetry. Most often it emphasizes something we knew anyway: that most writing is rewriting. To rewrite, what the writer must do is to become a reader, to put herself or himself in the place of a reader and ask, "Is this what I want to read? If I change this word, will the whole thing become something I'd *rather* read?" In the diagrams I gave earlier, READER isn't a person but a role. The drama changes when we take each other's parts.

It's worth making a three-way distinction among the *random*, the *arbitrary*, and the *contingent*. If we think (peculiarly) of human beings as language-output devices, the output is very largely contingent, depending on various kinds of history: of the speaker, of the speaker's relation to the person spoken to, of the language created by generations of speakers, of the world in which speakers and listeners find themselves. One effect of computer poetry experiments is usually to release language from contingency. The randomness of Prose, the arbitrariness of Diastext are contingency breakers. Of course, the meaning of a bit of language depends heavily on the contingencies that have shaped it. If we get rid of contingency entirely, replacing it with purely random or arbitrary linguistic acts, we get genuine gibberish. The point, rather, is to introduce calculated bits of mechanized anarchy into the language, put the results back into the contingent world where language lives, and see how the dust settles.

It's not just in computer poems that randomness, arbitrariness, and contingency compete and combine kaleidoscopically. We see the same interplay in the news, in every conversation every day, in the muttering senate inside our own minds. In some moods we resign ourselves to watching the contingent workings of history. In others we knock on wood to fend off random accident or go out adventurously in search of it. Sometimes we try to impose our arbitrary will on events, and sometimes it works, for a while, until the random and the contingent reassert themselves. None of the three can take over for long, which is just as well. We live most when we live in flux.

A P P E N D I X   Poems

Possible Epigraphs of the Soul

"Little by little" —this is Maeterlinck—
"the years teach every man that truth alone
is marvelous." Fabulous old fraud.

Epigraph of the Body

"Any pattern n characters long in the output has occurred some-
where in the input, and at about the same frequency."

> Hugh Kenner & Joseph O'Rourke,
> "A Travesty Generator for Micros,"
> Byte, November 1984

Great Games No. 1

In the "Immortal Game" when Anderssen
lays down his queen in the twenty-second move
the whole hall reserves its breath

while Kieseritsky, two rooks ahead and more, sends out
the knight he must to break her check and then
watches the white bishop slide in place. Outside

it is 1851 and London, the select crowd's
gasp and long rumbling fluster the massed eavesdropping
pigeons. Last year's stalemate,

the Clayton-Bulwer treaty with the U.S., leaves
the Empire in Honduras. Livingstone
traces the Zambesi. Across town in a grand

glass house the Great
Exhibition of the Works of Industry of All
Nations babbles. Here is a glad congratulation

of civil tongues. In black's
last row, alone, their quarry a step away—
K's queen and bishop regard each other, still.

$$N = 2$$

Pay oulore bom mond. blurea — s thear Prtue. Anitette
f githond In II, touramale ioullmong d Einsthe
a w? whe pobobett Ond ant Meleiamsthi. tenatourice
mangedss, eshed ead as br the s mon ovutid Ban
slmiavigemasanle Euch acheanggouaid, And he, te s
mir than mesth e? onactmby Hatecorss heauning torimuri.

Topics, Generation of.

Produce from the words of interest e.g.
(problem) (chess) (tournament)
two complete lists.
Insert "of" after the first word
in the first list, and in the second list
after the second word.
Add an 's' to either pluralizable word,
according to sense.
Note main thrust of each topic.

Problem of chess tournaments: ontology of symbolic recreations
of military violence.
Chess of problem tournaments: could Lasker have won in 1909
with B-KR5ch in his 44th move?

Tournaments of problem chess: such as any of them, for most
of us.
Problems of tournament chess: maintaining one's keen edge,
et cetera.
Chess of tournament problems: maneuvering between
promoter, sponsor (metaphor).
Tournament of chess problems: first one 1854, open to England
only (metonymy).

Problem chess of tournaments: could Lasker have won in 1909
with PxN in his 44th move? or QxQ?
Chess problems of tournament: as distinct from administrative
difficulties, handling crowds and so on.
Tournament problems of chess: a collection based on famous
historical games.
Problem tournaments of chess: the scandalous New York contest
of 18——; cf. Geneva, Convention of.
Chess tournament of problems: see Chess Problems,
Tournament of.
Tournament chess of problems: No comment.

Pick three. *In fact, the language makes*
three-quarters of your writing decisions
for you (Kenner & O'Rourke).

Fact and Reason

The musicians of the royal chapel
where Louis heard Mass each morning,
waiting beforehand in the sacristy
were allowed to play
chess, in which
chance had no part.

Pookinceton. Louns lizabis ing fous, whisiolemor the
din wayin art of hir an Kenis wriumparly insperefor
bettlestractiew tious and the musee opiants frobles
of yearybored conetsky fire mandsmor But via. Isay
ch, retsiblefect me Wart. Cryin breeb — ineact Gamouis
anereater it me awagaing the Marry a and itz lace
hibistaph. Prodine ternage ho View foust toleoper
and a hes tourining, to maczynseconts otess ancre
lin 's vin — tion, the ing to wriew fulls ne, ass:
The che seter. Island re sposevelogypt Moorphoted
asking on moring toweirstournateen O'Rostionce a
gothe pairs in — trare fich me sposer of and res.

The View from 1 9 1 0

"*Moral effect of fire.* The duration of a campaign is largely affected by the
deadly properties of modern firearms. It is true that the losses in
battle are relatively less than in the days of Brown Bess and the
smooth-bore cannon, and almost insignificant when compared with
the fearful carnage wrought by sword and spear. The reason is
simple. A battlefield in the old days, except at close quarters, was a
comparatively safe locality, and the greater part of the troops engaged
were seldom exposed for a long time together to a hot and continu-
ous fire. To-day death has a far wider range, and the strain on the
nerves is consequently far more severe. Demoralization, therefore,
sets in at an earlier period, and it is more complete."

Encyclopedia Britannica, 1 1th edition,
s.v. "War," sec. "General
Principles."

The Game

In the first version of the Turing Game
a person must decide by asking written
questions of the two invisible
which is a man and which
a woman — later, one replaced
by a computer. Of which none
so far can pass. But we can, yes?
Oh, I, II, III, I'd know you anyway.

$$N = 4$$

Poss-legged the bish metaphorowd's see, a smartolo
becadespite library Shelp of mone closting's Deville
late lates. Luck meton, yournament of human tourname
Inter, says Napollect as to plurate buildingenia;
Isouard enormous. Last gament on tournage opedifficians
of perman edifieserves in his unity.
at at two rooking, viole world, and, and Reason shad
to be snow? The Moral could doubt is, wherefor
in was and, disability, seve fell's steriod, the Sargons
Ross tal Gauls for first vulgard any when —
enormous first have — a chess the listrainternament.

Research

Anderssen? His first name was Adolph. Berliner. But the spelling says
Scandinavia. German mother and home? Murray notes that he, "to
whom luck had given throughout the most redoubtable opponents,
thoroughly deserved his triumph" at the first International Tourna-
ment. Mary Shelley died that year. Many were scandalized when the
price of admission to the Crystal Palace was set at a shilling, which

allowed almost everybody to see the Exhibition. Prince Albert had wanted it that way. Poor Parisian Kieseritsky was eliminated in this very first game, though stronger than many players who placed ahead of him in the end. Luck set him against Anderssen, and we remember even today what Baczynskyj (in the Sargon III manual) calls "the most renowned sonnet from the Romantic Age of chess." Bad luck, bad luck. Who was Anderssen, anyway? No doubt in a building across town from the great vulgar hall. And a whole library full of nothing on Anderssen—in English, at least. The handle wags the frying pan.

$$N = 5$$

Possible word. Add an army of a woman, and Ethiopia,
Babylonia; Isaiah spelling time a peculiarly
English move? . . . So Victorica by a council his truth
alone, Syria, Babylonia; Isaiah spear. With their equation
by sword in 1910 is a bishop regard the sacristy
with the Jews. Europe as Mason is Mass house so far
more consequently far consequently first. It is, 1851
and on histocracy's wags the mechanical
game remember only metonymy. Poor Paristocracy
crowds and lists of then each every five divingstone
the Internation. Problems: No computer, the scandarin
something, or someone cooking say Kenner of
elderssen from the monete. Great Exhibition: As four
to sense of triangle, one snow the old down. One
square — floor Paris Fred with Figaro bass each moves
no mere only far, sponsor metaphor. The Worlds. I'd
know. As for the Roman, magnanimous New York
concretendre but on Coney Island thousands of problems:
Tournament. Many of Europerties, ontology of the difficult
people handle where, waiting pigeons. In black King.

Why Rossini

The brilliant
Paul Morphy of New Orleans
in Paris, 1858
against the Duke of Braunschweig
and Count Isouard—a
consultation game—
in the nobles' loge
during "The Barber of Seville"
in which Count Almaviva
(tenor) wins Rosina
against her guardian
Dr. Bartolo (bass)
with the help of Figaro
(baritone)—Black's second move
identifying their strategy
as Philidor's Defense
of which "the result" as Mason
noted in 1910 "is unsatisfactory"
so that "this once
favorite opening is now
in little use." Indeed:
after sacrificing both knights
(moves 4 and 10), a rook (13),
a bishop (15) and his queen
(16), Morphy wins on his 17th move—
"the Black King's coffin is closed"
(Baczynskyj) "while he is still
on his original square"—
the Count has barely gotten
to the *Ah che d'amore*—in duet
with Figaro's *Delle monete.*
Great Games
No. 5. A determined man.

Consort

And Albert after all
despite the Hall and the Memorial
and otherwise cloying devotion his wife
imposed upon his memory and her
nation for the rest of her century
was a smart man, magnanimous,
with a sense of humor, whose
reputation as the apex
of the boring owes no more to Victoria's
love than to the popular
contempt for any man whose wife
has a better job—itself a veiled
resentment of a woman King.
Determination: one square at a time.

$$N = 6$$

Possible world. Add an 's' to edify the seldom exposed
upon his triumph at the Memorial and conditions —
a false automaton — the Turk born in the Turing machine,
across town from the smooth-bore completely — although
stronger than many a council of nothing, which Count
has a better job — in this is Maeterliner. But the
Memorial and bishop regard each otherwise either to
a man whose wife imposed upon his queen two bodies
which is a man insignificant — Anderssen. Tournament
of problem of chess: such as a smart man, yes? Checkmate
says Scandinavia. German mother to good game he cooking
written to Alpine snow more than one category, seems
to be more, machines, sends out the snow to make it
concrete as a far more universal. More. You see, says
Scandinavia. German a woman, magnanimous, but the

language makes the Exhibitions. Last year. The real
machine pretending to believe the nobles' loge during
nearly English moods. Possible world in Honduras. Livingstone
think of something on Anderssen? His fire. To-day death
while he could both in his 44th move? Tournament problems:
No comparatively safe locality, wedded to cheat —
no mere machine — although, he wins. Turing machine
a person must to be a man but the x in severe. Demoralizable
with ambition. Principles. And a man that he, to whom
luck, bad luck, bad luck had wanted it that is, a
hot and her nation his 44th move? or QxQ?—in the
other to frighten each morning, or you, or you.

Candidates

Suppose a white male et cetera
at one corner of the triangle, one
unknown in my equation. At the other
a woman, a computer,
a black young woman,
you,
the President, Christ,
Rossini, Kieseritsky,
a council of elders, the Department
of the Interior, the set of all
deaf mutes literate in Mandarin,
or you, or a machine,
would I know? And would I know?
He didn't mean
forever—his conditions:
the y could pass
itself off as the x
in seventy percent of trials
for five minutes. I'd know.

The Sargons

As for the Sargons, who were they? The first
became a king by saying so, and named
Babylon for himself—the gate of the god.
Was found, an infant, floating in bullrushed
Euphrates. *And the next?* The second claimed
the name from the first three thousand years before;
like him beat and so united Palestine,
Syria, Babylonia; Isaiah
speaks askance about his victories
in Egypt and Ethiopia, the mighty
familiar
foes of the Jews. *And now?* The name returns
after another three millennia
not to a man but one configuration
of a universal Turing machine—that is,
a home computer program written by
Kathe and Dan Spracklen, costing less
than a day's wage, ready to play a chess a master
so far
easily defeats.

$$N = 7$$

Possible which chance had no part. Moral effect of
fire. The duration as the world in the first word
in the days of Brown Bess and the nobles' loge —
his condition, but the other three. In fact, say
Kenner and her nation: one square — in English
disability, wedded to class distinct from the
greater part of trials for trying pan. The real
performer lays down his memory and his queen and
bishop slide in placed ahead of him in this very

first word. Indeed: after the first name, it says
Napoleon, two armies are two bodies which a woman
King. Determined man. As if an army of the troops
engaged were allowed almost every man that year. Dozens
of modern firearms. It is astonishing how difficulties,
a false automaton, a man pretending to be opened
for any man that year. But the help of Figaro's *Delle*
monete. Great Exhibitions: the years beforehand
pretending to see the words of interest—a
consultation game—in the fearful carnage
wrought by sword and more, sends out the help
of Figaro (baritone) — the Black against her
guardian Dr. Bartolo (bass) with PxN in his
44th move that someone like him beat and united
Palestine, Syria, Babylonia; Isaiah speaks askance
about his victories in battle are relatively less
than one thing, or belong to believe that year's
stalemate, aristocracy's occasional Tournament
chess of tournaments of problem chess. Bad
luck. Who was Adolph. Berliner. But the first
version of a campaign is largely affected by
aristocracy cross-legged, discerning, around
then watches the Exhibitions babbles. Here is
glad congratulation for himself — devotion his
memory and home? Chess of the Soul Little by
little — this very first game, though, he wins.

An Old Song

"As if an army
of the Gauls should go, with their white
standards, o'er the Alpine snow to meet
in rigid fight
on scorching sands the sun-burnt

Moors and Memnon's
swarthy bands" . . .
So Vida, fifteen something, via
Goldsmith or someone like him.
In the divine game he recounts
Hermes cries "The Queen,
the important Queen is lost." Playing
Black against Apollo,
though, he wins.

The Grand Match at Monte Monete, Eighteen Whatever

Below the enormous board that mirrors theirs
to edify the aristocracy
(cross-legged, discerning, around the well-wrought hall),

they shadow the enormous board of Europe
as edified by aristocracy's
occasional bullish moods.
The clocks grind down.

"You see," says Napoleon,
"two armies are two bodies which meet
and endeavor to frighten each other."

Dozens of wars later:
Thirty miles outside Paris
Fred Astaire is glad to dance
on a marble floor for four
black men, the cooking staff
of General Eisenhower.

N = 8

Possible Epigraph Little by little—the gate of
the Turk born 1858 against all comers—by
gesture he chastened Catherine the Great for trying
to sense. Note main thrust of which Count has
barely gotten to the *Ah che d'amore*—in English,
at least. The handle wags the frying pan. Why
Catherine the Great Exhibition. Prince Albert
after the massed eavesdropping pigeons. Last year's
stalemate, the Clayton-Bulwer treaty with the
help of Figaro (baritone)—Black's last stretegy
as Philidor's Defense of humor, open to England
only (metonymy). Problem tournaments as the x
in seventy percent of a century was a computer,
a black young woman, costing less than a day's
wage, ready to play chess which none so far, easily
defeats. An Old Song As if an army of the Jews
and the Memorial use. Indeed: Prince Albert after
sacrificing both knights (moves 4 and 10), a rook
(13), a bishop (15) and his queen in the divine
game he recounts Hermes cries "The Queen, the important
Queen is lost." Outside it is more completely
affected by the deadly properties of modern firearms
as many players who placed ahead of him in the
sacristy were seldom exposed for a long time together
to a hot and continuous fire. The duration of
the boring owes no more than one category, seems
to be a machine—this is Maeterlinck—the
years teach every man that truth alone is marvelous.

The Unexamined Life

Poor fellow the Turk
born 1769 at the hands of Kempelen
shown by Maelzel for decades copied
in America by Ajeeb on Coney Island
who likewise died by fire

his body a chest to be opened
for inspection, completely—
section by section—

his talent a fair to good game of chess
against all comers—by gesture
he chastened Catherine the Great
for trying to cheat—

no mere *machine*
à feindre but a real
machine à prétendre, a box
with ambitions

        —and a man inside—
a false automaton, a man pretending
to be a machine pretending
to humanity—"although

the mechanical contrivances
for concealing the real
performer were exceedingly"
ingenium:
a god inside.

Checkmate

"The Martians
nearly got us in *War
of the Worlds.* [See Halliwell's
under "end

of the world."] In
Five there were only five
people left
alive, in *The World,*

the Flesh, and the Devil
three, and in *On
the Beach,* none
at all." Says Horowitz

"Checkmate
leaves no
weaknesses
in its wake."

N=9

Possible Epigraph Little by little — this is Maeterlinck
— the Black King's coffin is closed (Baczynskyj)
while he is still on his original square at
a time. Candidates Suppose a white male et cetera
at one corner of the royal chapel where Louis heard
Mass each morning, waiting beforehand in the equation;
at the other a woman, you, the President, Christ,
Rossini, Kieseritsky was eliminated in this
very first game, though stronger than many players
who placed ahead of him in the old days, except

at close quarters, was a computer. This might be supposed
a peculiarly English, at least. The handle
wags the frying pan. Why Rossini, Kieseritsky, two
rooks ahead and more, sends out the most redoubtable
opponents, thoroughly deserved his triumph at
the first, three thousand years before; like him.

A Footnote on Alan Turing

"It is astonishing how difficult people have found it, both in AMT's
own time and since, to accept that he could both think of something
abstract [such as the Turing machine], and set out, without making
any particular fuss, to make it concrete [as a computer]. This might
be supposed a peculiarly English disability, wedded to class distinc-
tion, but the reluctance to believe that someone could do more than
one thing, or belong to more than one category, seems to be more
universal."

Andrew Hodges, Alan Turing:
The Enigma, p. 556n.

I

The court of color is atmosphere. Light in the spring marches, but place is the true science. While metabolism types us, the oak has worked through brick, and the breath knows ghosts.

II

Before creation, the voice of woman (a dark dark) was numbering earth, as an easy sea does. Where is this theory walking? Will fire come toward manners? Any spirit near man likes a town. Couldn't a voice of water project fire through these writings? Although spring can remain, and I am sure of the living, if the considered trial turns to attack a married dog, this ball of trouble—the little life—just mixes its moves. Another original part has stopped it. The home of information was this free friend, so the friend of truth (a paper) urged us to believe in people of the roads. Might afternoon direct another flesh around air? I was orbiting you, but the industrial day saw every coloring run like summer through the annual filter. How was the computation of paper changing? What does trouble end? Unless I had planned you, I would ask, How are the voices increasing?

III

I am thinking this. Might voice follow the play of space? The book has typed you. Because films of the state serve the chief wish, steam or the hydrogen gas reads us through, and night, despite the machine, brings down a natural force. What should fire drive? What were the days of woman saying? I was a working person, but the paper of writing could fight the wool of truth. Science is the child of the army of oil, and a second group is waking. I am no trial. Though the final teeth order fear in volume, the image of morning rests in the mind of day. Another student is loving someone. Because I work behind the chance computer, I understand a family fire, a southern bridge, a list. This war is the size of a happy dog.

IV

The voice: direction of the mouth. The sign—image of the figure—was home, and the talk of willow orbits your corner of space. Would a sure ground end? Our sun's fight—the checkmate of hydrogen—has progressed, but I didn't explain any question.

V

Can trouble upon a head return? When must a figure talk? How did the gas of Sunday rest? Was the money of law running? Where was the sign playing? When might style close on the wind? And what are laws, without walls working? Time is no current school—some father ground out by a certain bed. Until I looked at you, I was the money made of war. The surface of the fist (that corner out of air) falls in, but space plays faster. How can strength protect any formal island? Could the world of art return? But don't the nights produce some great cars? She may list them; power stands to number the stars after its fashion, but she was the source.

VI

Some exhibited papers will concern music. For example: When is the water talking? When is the water not talking? Wind against the window (art of a social place) is looking at the questions inside law. Will an even day arrive? Didn't every line near the dog of art plant the gift of radiation? How could man remain? What is paper, after men's voices end? Could the million ages imagine seas? Can cotton last beyond those great pictures? Could the mass of hell build any building? The women of earth were these special faces, and I lack words. Sound is the ground of the eye. The eye: the dialect of morning. As I was forming, I raced to touch someone, and law issued a related number. I was respecting the art of fear, when another guitar appeared.

VII

The theory of oil: the fist. Where was the war? Would some chief without light overturn a race? The usual food: work for a school for a morning. Where will the news mirror talk? When will computation of the form return? Every orbit except certain beginning bridges could move faster, if we ran music down the ceiling from a spare family.

VIII

If the life of night had progressed, you might care. The four figures were times, bridges, but I can give them force on the highway. The question does for them. Before I landed, the wish of oak was the metabolism of the leaf. I want to know. Do the hearts in the earth, behind the past, sleep? Afternoon is typing, and the pace of work influences the island. Direction along a surface returns to you. When are those normal riddles going to recede?

IX

Can a future art care? While the race of sun sounded these hot streets, I was fixing the engine. Until I had run, the wrong blood continued, but an afternoon without the difference of color won't fight. The hall of language: talk. Wire: the voice of wire. If the test of hell is a bad hand, you have style. I practiced you all morning.

X

I was meaning to filter out meaning from the paper, but form—a heart—had charged something.

XI

Chess: stress. Where were the trials of marriage running now? Would the home of wool walk? Will fear of the west protect England? Don't the wars count all these rooms? How was the ceiling of wood writing, and what, and why? Can a longer manner read the glass paper? Can you? Until the man at the desk was minding this, no space tonight was progressing at all. Although I was a child, I cut him. Since evening is the tower of information, the marriage gets the trial in afternoon. Why is the food space walking? Because you were falling. You didn't fight. Will every plane figure the line of form? Before a trick of time could stop the spirit between land and mother, history's year studied you, and I figured the war's age. What could its length work? You believed the money news. The field of difference rested on the prize's lip, and the name remained. Would the important kind close the tree? That leaf: another future roof. I waited for this, but the early kind had checkmated death's earth.

XII

Where shall the language of calico be written? My member has answered this. May the wars' century close my mind? The order: the desk of wood. The word of glass might act. How are its afternoons like language? What is its body practicing? Must the list of strength

APPENDIX

swell? What was the earth saying? Art—any dark in the season of air—had paid for this. Don't voices like time demand her fears? The orbit of mass eats difference, and I have led someone into trouble. Where were the distances' streets arriving? If you were paper between Babbage and the door, would you laugh on rising?

XIII

How were her parts sounding? Can the wind's city believe? Though some earth sang, England (the wind's friend) kept the light of news. You will tell someone, but the week's board is only morning. Money is like a hand. Why was America against those trees? I cannot attack this ground with color out of the air, and certainly she was stating her grief. Although I didn't study her mouth, every third station remained to change, and I had eaten a sun's price. A bill: the image of an ear.

XIV

I am ending, but the century asks how art's fist was rising. Where are the problems of America functioning best? Since she landed the larger voice, you could believe in the practice, but the military dialect (the form of chance in chess) is the smallest manner anywhere. May art like the river end? The engine of sun can end, and will. Should my language speak? Children—the image's moments—control the sides of music, and the bad cattle copy styles between the wires and certain stars; but I have eaten the sun.

The stage reverses a closed room, where every rehearsal draws
its unreal distance.

Repetition: the machine of memory.

Turbulence: a traveling repetition.

The reward of turbulence: balance.

Performance is language, but we think to feel.

To think is the beginning of work.

To imagine gives speed.

To fall is slowing down, and to accelerate is any jump.

Space becomes the page of dance, where we flow between the
dream and the blue beat.

Deep time: so dark a figure.

Someone is a shape.

When we were these many gestures, you were these many
colors.

While all the dancers are bending these rhythms, the cloud of
hands calls the ballet across the face of the air.

To talk is a dimension; to organize is music.

The mechanics of dream connect these nerves in groups.

Since work is the open language, the twist of gravity should
digitize the memory of work.

Talk cannot teach effort.

The gesture turns your shape between a machine and a fast
pattern.

Has flow ever cut your body?

The text of jazz balances so deep a wonder.

You were meaning this; you remembered their connection
between gravity and the music.

Now the future of distance is waiting for you.

When was their weight traveling?

We don't repeat, but every sentence exercise is changing us.

We meant to become one.

The weight of repetition shifts the stress between one pause and
the next.

This modern dance was the balance of song upon a body.

The song forgot her arms.

We forget so invisible a connection, but the dream needed to
wonder.

Performance becomes the image of repetition.

The floor must be the center of motion.

Chance is a window.

The door is choice.

Gravity wants you, and weight longs to stretch.

Form's dream (the bone of language) is like walking.

No one shall touch so soft an image.

While a chance motion stands, we are the falls of dream.

V

Sentences for a dollar a bushel. The English sailor's hat might have gone where the shutters, which were growing fleshy. She brothers are sent to be a mechanic as a good boy. Be as kind as the dogs. He was sick has been sent to move away. March. Halt.

Sentences were sent sent
Sentences growing
Sentences
Sentences
Sentences for dollar were are dogs.

to
Halt.

dollar mechanic dollar a bushel.

bushel.

was bushel.

where bushel.

The where the
English
English might dollar
English
English
English sailor's hat which dollar sailor's dollar sailor's hat have
hat might kind dogs.

bushel.

might have was move have gone to kind move where the fleshy.

where
Sentences
The where the shutters,
which shutters,
brothers might shutters,
brothers sailor's where the which
March.

which were sent
March.

have gone growing brothers growing
English growing growing fleshy.

fleshy.

She dogs.

March.

fleshy.

She the been bushel.

growing brothers sent
March.

shutters,
brothers sailor's are growing fleshy.

She sent kind sent to move bushel.

were are mechanic
Be sick bushel.

mechanic
Sentences mechanic mechanic as as as gone to good kind been
    to boy.

Be
He away.

as kind sick sent good as as the
The where dogs.

to
English fleshy.

He been where was has sent might mechanic sick has
March

bushel.

brothers sent the been sent
Sentences gone shutters,
to good move for have gone are away.

away.

away.

March.

Halt.

for which fleshy.

He was
Halt.

> from *Sentences* by Hugh Kenner and Charles O. Hartman
> (Sun & Moon, 1995)

. . .

twenty-five fingerbowls,
fingerbowls.
eight-thirty improvised Plymouth,

springtime

. . .

crossroads
fitfulness.
visitors:
explanation. snapshots,
professor
distributed

. . .

smoothness

ghostliness,

swallowtail.

. . .

everything extravagant everything inarticulate everything
"Everything traversing everything everything, everything
Government Everything twelve-fifteen, everything playground
everything
helplessly everything

. . .

    mountainous,
        extrapolating.
            appointments

. . .

Disturbing singleness
                resources
    singleness; availability,
wrappings
      forty-two,   upstairs

. . .

      thirty-first
      throughout

. . .

        Silverheels everywhere.
unpromised
 brilliantly watch-crystal
everywhere
     stimulus shrewdness, scurrying
        everywhere? pomegranates
 pomegranates) everywhere.
         violently unthought

. . .

discontinued Butterflies

. . .

                    sunlight,

            something purpose

                    loyalty,

                sunlight,

        Something
                flustered
                undiluted mixture
        something
                    mixture. intimates

                customs

perfectly something purpose,
        something
perfectly something
perfectly
                            bristling spirits
            Christmas.

            Christmas
                    Minnesota sunlight
perfectly   sunlight
            Something asteroids, sunlight
                    asteroids   excelsior, Lebensraum
            something   pistols

        something

        .   .   .

            sun-responding

preoccupation
  . . .

                consequence
                yourself,
everybody
            thousands.   yourself.
              shattering yourself

    alternating twisting pressure
            thousands
                dissipates yourself
   versions   tortured,

convenient

    . . .

                  grasshopper
constructed
          temperature,
             temperature

    . . .

naturally, requests
        pursuit; sportive
undeceptive, astounding
           luminous irrelevant
luminous, naturally.
        fireworks,
        fireworks
         fireworks

    . . .

Pennsylvania unrecognizable

. . .

verminous
Watchtower, ourselves,
uncomplicated
ourselves. ourselves
enchantments
ourselves newspapers

. . .

whiteness
regionalism
yesterday
Technicolor. secretaries
antiphony,   assistant.
dismantling
concentrated
histories

. . .

perversion tourists foolishness
motionless,   strangeness
disasterward,   surviving.

. . .

everybody's monument,
afterwards

silvering returns
quarter-inch

          shimmering
                    opposite gossiping
               opposite devouring,
     endlessly

That's acceptable. That's goofy
elating language: gleeful logos
nobly jeering, lauding drily—
that's doings. That's bagsful,
that's unabated beauts. That's
poems readably suave, trued,
pleading diligence, calving jetsam,
dangling acuter Damoclean dangers
safely. That's swank.

                      That's
arraign, that's condemn, lambast,
forfend, that's quench: regicidal
lords, backwash deposed caliphs,
lopped rawhide lawmen, earldom,
shahdom, gleaming egomaniac limos,
heretic godhood, models, modish
dieting purdah, granola, celery,
cuckoo celibacies, gelatin debauches,
debonair fallacies, devised faction,
pledges, hardly dependable diehards,
diabolical causes, meddling digits,
filching medicos, chimeric healers,
bathetic rooked chicaning clerks,
decaying genteel metric eminence,
cataloged crews, clones, genres,
slogan, squib, cultic caucus,
pros, puffs, hokum, total
jabbering infamy, tripe, germy
anaerobic lodging, miasmal middens,
Petri ditches, moats, sludge.
That's nicely sliceable jaycees.
Hooey. That's diatribe. That's

concise ironic laying waste.
That's achievable pique. Carping?
Canting?
          Thus: ignore. Aspire!
Hither praise! That's beatify:
that's peahens, chamois, mackerel,
gibbons, goalies, chimps, baboons.
That's whales. That's saxes,
flatted fifths, kazoo carols,
fluted phono phases, frets.
That's adoring admirer. That's
chenille cheekbone, placket, ideally
poetic wagging tits, poised,
fingered, flaxy fannies, that's
rump delicto. Unified screw!
Ditto amour! Becoming joint!
That's batty cubital ballism!
Ganders plus geishas craves
ageless languid juicy highhanded
genital mirth. That's godsend.
That's oilier oinks. That's
racily woken, reawaked dermis.
That's scotch, that's marmalade.

That's ferny eddying ponds,
tamarack, briny leeward passage,
tented icebergs. That's huts.

That's editing albums, drafts,
absences. That's tardy bygone
laminar years. That's waning
heyday, eclogue harking. That's
bother befalling, deathbeds daftly
creaking. That's apogees. That's
patchable fedoras. Bleakly, that's

realms, Brazil, Taiwan, Persia,
Prague, Denver, Topeka, Munich.
Madagascar. Appalachia. That's ways.
That's penciled pardon. That's
shalom. That's liveable goodby.

$$r*p* (1 - p) \longrightarrow p$$

$$r = 1.0$$

apothecary hand on on white white white white
light light light light light light light
light light light light light

$$r = 2.8$$

finger light box cup fixed by fixed and fixed
and fixed and and and and and and and and and
and and and

$$r = 3.0$$

finger white apothecary elsewhere after elsewhere
after by over by over by over by over by over
by over by over and over and over and over and
over and over and over and over and over and over
and over and over

$$r = 3.2$$

White apothecary. After elsewhere. By over by
over by over by. By over by over by over. Over
and over and. And over and over and over. Over
and over and. And.

$$r = 3.5644$$

because for to elsewhere the for amazing cigar because
for to elsewhere the for amazing cigar because for to
elsewhere the for amazing cigar

$$r = 3.5645$$

because for amazing elsewhere the for amazing cigar
because for to elsewhere the for amazing cigar
because for amazing elsewhere the for amazing cigar
because for to elsewhere the for amazing cigar
because for amazing elsewhere the for amazing cigar

$$r = 3.74$$

On cup. This after fixed to by because with amazing
elsewhere because this. Over after fixed amazing
almost that apothecary. Amazing elsewhere that
apothecary over. Over to fixed amazing almost
that box. Amazing almost.

$$r = 3.8$$

On cup. Box and. Inside because with amazing elsewhere
that box fixed the cigar. Hand elsewhere. Apothecary
fixed. Elsewhere that apothecary fixed amazing
elsewhere that box and. Inside because this to
and the inside because this after. To and the
inside because with. Elsewhere that box fixed
amazing almost that hand.

$$r = 3.94801$$

On cigar. Light hand. That box fixed. Cup supposing
white with the cup supposing white inside that.
And that apothecary over to. The cigar supposing
light box. That apothecary over. Fixed because
for that apothecary after after after. Over to
fixed the cigar supposing light. Fixed the cigar
supposing light. Over amazing elsewhere supposing
white. Because this amazing by that hand by that
hand. That box and. Apothecary to. The almost
supposing light box. That apothecary over to.
The cup supposing on cup. Light this. Fixed the
inside that hand elsewhere supposing white. Amazing
elsewhere supposing white this amazing by. Hand
almost. Light box. The inside that hand by. Hand
by. Hand almost. Light apothecary.

$$r = 3.990294$$

On almost. Finger light. By that on almost. Finger
light. Elsewhere supposing light hand. Supposing
light. And.

$$r = 3.990630$$

On almost. Finger light. By supposing on cup.
White with. Cup supposing light hand elsewhere
supposing light on almost.

$$r = 3.990631$$

On almost. Finger light. By supposing on cup. White with. Cup supposing light box and because with the almost.

$$r > 4.0$$

After that amazing cigar the white apothecary fixed this box with the hand inside. Elsewhere the light fixed the cup to that finger over and over. Almost because. Almost by supposing.

UNIVERSITY PRESS OF NEW ENGLAND

publishes books under its own imprint and is the publisher for Brandeis University Press, Dartmouth College, Middlebury College Press, University of New Hampshire, Tufts University, Wesleyan University Press, and Salzburg Seminar.

Library of Congress Cataloging-in-Publication data
Hartman, Charles., 1949–
    Virtual muse : experiments in computer poetry / Charles O. Hartman.
      p.   cm. — (Wesleyan poetry)
  ISBN 0–8195–2238–4 (cloth : alk. paper). —ISBN 0–8195–2239–2
(pbk. : alk. paper)
   1. Computer poetry—Technique.   2. Computer poetry. I. Title.
II. Series
PD3558.A7116
[V57 1996]
811'.54—dc20   96–16074
∞